Educational Psychology Casebook

PATRICIA P. WILLEMS
Florida Atlantic University

ALYSSA R. GONZALEZ-DEHASS
Florida Atlantic University

PEARSON

Boston   New York   San Francisco
Mexico City   Montreal   Toronto   London   Madrid   Munich   Paris
Hong Kong   Singapore   Tokyo   Cape Town   Sydney

Senior Editor: *Arnis E. Burvikovs*
Editorial Assistant: *Kelly Hopkins*
Marketing Manager: *Kris Ellis-Levy*
Production Editor: *Greg Erb*
Editorial Production Service: *Publishers' Design and Production Services, Inc.*
Manufacturing and Composition Buyer: *Andrew Turso*
Electronic Composition: *Publishers' Design and Production Services, Inc.*
Cover Administrator: *Kristina Mose-Libon*

For related titles and support materials, visit our online catalog at www.ablongman.com.

Between the time website information is gathered and then published, it is not unusual for some sites to have closed. Also, the transcription of URLs can result in typographical errors. The publisher would appreciate notification where these errors occur so that they may be corrected in subsequent editions.

Library of Congress Cataloging-in-Publication Data

Willems, Patricia P.
    Educational psychology casebook / Patricia P. Willems, Alyssa R. Gonzalez-DeHass.
        p. cm.
    ISBN 0-205-43897-0 (alk. paper)
        1. Educational psychology—United States—Case studies.
    I. Gonzalez-DeHass, Alyssa R. II. Title.

LB1051.W589 2006
370.15—dc22   2005048921

Printed in the United States of America

10 9 8 7 6 5 4 3   CST   10 09 08 07

To our husbands for always listening and
to our parents for always believing,
we thank you for your loving support of our dreams.

Contents

Preface

This book is a product of our collaboration for wanting to create a helpful tool for professors and instructors of educational psychology. We teach undergraduates and graduates in the field of educational psychology in an institution where a field experience for the courses is not required. Thus, we wanted students to be able to ground the theoretical framework of educational psychology in a real-life context. While the cases do not attempt to replace actual classroom experience, they are a helpful way to embed students in the culture of the classroom by bringing the contextual examples to them.

The cases are organized into six major parts: Human Development, Individual Differences and Diversity, Learning Theories, Motivation, Classroom Management, and Assessment and Evaluation. Each part contains cases that address specific topics particular to that subject matter. The cases have been deliberately written without a conclusion so as to allow students to engage in critical thinking, problem solving, role playing, analysis, and decision making. We felt that in leaving the cases open-ended, it would allow for flexibility in how they are used and thus would give the professor or instructor more autonomy in how they would like to use the case studies in the classroom.

Ten of the cases were written to include one of the video clips in MyLabSchool. MyLabSchool is a suite of online tools located at www.mylabschool.com, to which professors, instructors, and students will have access with the purchase of this book. In particular, MyLabSchool allows students to observe real classrooms in action in a variety of grade levels and school settings through the use of video clips. While these cases can be used independently of the video clips, we felt that this was an added feature that would incorporate a visual component to complement the text.

KEY FEATURES

- The book contains a simple Contents that allows for a quick glance at the topics covered in each case as well as the range of ages that the case addresses.
- The book also contains a detailed listing of cases at the beginning of each part that features a brief synopsis of each case and identifies whether the case is accompanied by one of the video clips found in MyLabSchool. Thus, professors and instructors can use technology in their classrooms as part of their case-study instruction.
- Each case contains a section at the beginning that lists the theoretical or topical areas covered in the case and identifies whether the case can be used in conjunction with one of the video clips. The professor or instructor can then select which case they would want to use with each of their lessons.
- At the end of each case, there are questions and topics for discussion that cover the case as well as the theories or topics addressed in the case. This may help professors or instructors in using the cases in the way that they feel most align with their teaching of the subject area.
- There is a list of suggested outside readings at the end of the casebook, which contains journal articles, books, conference proposals, and so on that are pertinent to the subject area of each case and that allow the professor or instructor to extend discussion beyond the case.

- The book contains two matrixes. One matrix links each of the cases to the Educator Accomplished Practices, and the other matrix aligns each case with the Praxis II. This feature is meant to aid professors and instructors who want a connection between their instruction and regional or national standards.

ACKNOWLEDGMENTS

We would like to thank the following individuals for reviewing and commenting on the manuscript: Jane Benjamin, Mansfield University; Daniel Fasko, Bowling Green State University; Terri Flowerday, University of New Mexico; James Furukawa, Towson University; Cheryl Greenberg, University of North Carolina–Greensboro; Pamela Guess, University of Tennessee at Chattanooga; Darlene Hoffman, Millikin University; Dan Hursh, West Virginia University; Yuliang Liu, Southern Illinois University; David Magleby, Brigham Young University–Idaho; Ken Springer, Southern Methodist University; and Ron Zigler, Pennslyvania State University.

PART I
Human Development

CASE 1: Another Typical Day

Synopsis: A description of a series of events that take place in a kindergarten teacher's typical day.

CASE 2: Resolutions

Synopsis: After the schoolwide implementation of conflict managers for conflict interventions, a fifth-grade teacher decides to extend the use of such managers to her own classroom. With the help of student conflict managers as well as through her own interventions, this teacher resolves disputes and teaches social skills.

 ## VIDEO CLIP 2: Social Skills Development

Video Synopsis: Mrs. Harrington, an elementary school principal, has decided to create a group of students called conflict managers to handle disputes that occur on the playground. Conflict managers are trained to handle minor incidents before they escalate into severe behavioral issues.

CASE 3: Reaching Out

Synopsis: A third-grade teacher is concerned about one of his students whose parents are going through divorce. The student's classroom behavior and academic performance have become enough of a concern that the teacher is now considering contacting parents for a parent–teacher conference.

CASE 4: Choices

Synopsis: A middle school student coerced by a friend faces the consequences of his decision to cheat after his first exam grade is less than stellar.

CASE 5: Identity Lost

Synopsis: An eleventh grader grapples with issues of popularity, relationships, and parental restraints.

Another Typical Day

Suggested Theories/Content: Cognitive Development, Classroom Management, and Psychosocial Development

Noah is on the playground with his class during recess. He realizes his shoe is untied so he attempts to tie it. After several attempts, he asks Mrs. Arling, his teacher, to help him. As she ties his shoe she sings a song about a bunny, which she hopes will help him remember how to tie his shoe. "Noah, are you listening to the song?" asks Mrs. Arling. "Yeah, it is like the song that my mommy sings about little bunny foo-foo!" he replies excitedly. "Well, it is about a bunny, Noah, but this song is a little bit different, the words are to help you remember how to tie your shoe," Mrs. Arling replies gently. "It is just like bunny foo-foo," replies Noah. "Noah, it is not like bunny foo-foo, I know that song too because I sing it to my son . . ." Noah interrupts Mrs. Arling and asks in amazement, "You have a son?" "Yes, Noah, I have told the class that many times. His name is Richard and he is thirteen." "Oh, yeah, that. I just thought you were telling me that you are a mommy but you aren't 'cause you are our teacher!" Noah says with excitement as he runs happily toward the other children now that his shoe is tied. Mrs. Arling grins in amusement; after all, she knows that she will have to continue tying his shoes for a bit longer.

Just then Mrs. Arling overhears a conversation some of her students are having. "Myron did not cheat, cheating is when you take pieces off the board and hide them and then use them later!" says Margo. "Yeah, but he ran around the monkey bars and not under them like we were supposed to and that is cheating!" exclaims Russell. "No, it isn't because he did not take anything!" cries Margo. The students then all agree with Margo and continue to play. Since the students resolved this problem themselves, Mrs. Arling decides to check on Kyle, who normally is always engaged in some activity with his classmates, but who today is sitting by himself. When Mrs. Arling questions Kyle, he tells her that he would like to play with the other children, but he accidentally brought "Lambchop," his toy lamb, to school today and he does not want to leave him by himself—after all, he does not want Lambchop to be lonely. "How about if I take Lambchop and keep him with me while you play?" replies Mrs. Arling. "Yeah! Thanks, Mrs. Arling!" replies Kyle excitedly; he then kisses Lambchop and rushes off to join his friends.

Later that day, Mrs. Arling has her teacher's aide help the students with their math lesson. She has the students grouped by their abilities, although it is difficult since what they can perform without guidance changes rapidly. Mrs. Arling instructs Anna, her assistant, that she may help the students with their assignments, answer questions, and provide any guidance that they need; however, she is not to give them the answers nor is she to solve the problems for them. Mrs. Arling also instructs her to place a check mark next to the student's name indicating that she provided them with assistance on this task. Mrs. Arling explains to Anna that the check marks will inform her of what the students can accomplish independently and what they needed assistance with.

Luke and Margo, who are part of one group, begin to quarrel over the bin filled with colored pencils that is in the center of their table. "Margo! I was using the green, give it back, it's mine!" Luke yells. "No, it is mine now, use something else!" shouts Margo. Mrs. Arling interrupts the argument by saying "OK, let's not argue, we all need to share the pencils. Now, Margo, give Luke back the color he was using and then you may use it when he is finished." Margo replies in a whiny tone, "But Mrs. Arling I want it now! Now! And he will just take forever with it." "I am sorry, Margo, but you will have to wait your turn. How would you like it if Luke took something you were using and refused to give it back?" Mrs. Arling asks softly. "I dunno, I just want the green back!" Margo exclaims as she begins to cry. "Well, why don't we see if another group has an extra green pencil that they can share with you?" asks Mrs. Arling. "Yes," replies Margo immediately wiping the tears from her face.

Later that day the class is taking part in their "treat of the day," which is something special that the students engage in if they have been good all week. Ella, who is new to the class, doesn't know what the "treat of the day" is; she wonders if she should ask Mrs. Arling, but instead she decides to wait and see what the other children do. After all, Ella thinks, it has the word *treat* in it and that, Ella knows, is always a good thing! She soon discovers she is correct for it is something good. This week the students are watching a movie while they eat a snack. Suddenly Luke stands up and exclaims irritably, "Hey, Russell got more than me!" Mrs. Arling calmly replies, "Luke, Russell has two brownies because his brownies are very small, when you place his two brownies side by side they are the same size as the one you got." Luke seems puzzled; however, before he has a chance to respond, other students begin to complain about Russell getting two brownies. Mrs. Arling decides to go around the room and cut all of the large brownies into two pieces. Soon all of the students are happy and quickly go back to watching the movie. Mrs. Arling smiles; after all, it is just another typical day in her kindergarten class.

DISCUSSION TOPICS

1. Cognitive Development

    a. According to Piaget, identify the stage of cognitive development that the students are likely to be in.

    b. Illustrate instances in the case that demonstrate Piaget's concept of assimilation and/or accommodation.

    c. Relate instances in the case that demonstrate a child's schema.

    d. Explain how Piaget's concept of egocentrism is apparent in this case.

    e. Discuss an instance where conservation is demonstrated by the students in this case.

    f. Summarize other Piagetian concepts demonstrated by the students in this case.

    g. Judge whether Mrs. Arling understands her students' cognitive development. Support your answer with examples from the case.

    h. Explain how Vygotsky's concept of scaffolding is demonstrated in this case.

    i. Discuss an instance in the case that involves the zone of proximal development.

    j. Conclude whether Mrs. Arling is using Vygotsky's sociocontextual theory effectively in her class. Support your answer with examples from the case.

2. Classroom Management

    a. Evaluate Mrs. Arling on her classroom management strategy. Determine her effectiveness.

    b. Explain whether Mrs. Arling demonstrates "withitness" in the classroom. Support your answer with examples from the case.

    c. Describe some of the appropriate management methods that teachers can employ for this grade level.

3. Erikson's Stages of Psychosocial Development

    a. Which stage of Erikson's stages of psychosocial development are the students likely to be in? How is that demonstrated in the case?

b. Conclude whether Mrs. Arling is aiding her students for the positive resolution of the "crisis" that, according to Erikson, children experience in this stage.

c. Generate strategies that aid students in this age group with psychosocial development.

CASE 2

Resolutions

 VIDEO: Social Skills Development
located at *mylabschool.com*

Suggested Theories/Content: Social Development, Psychosocial Development, Social Cognitive Theory, and Cognitive Development

Mrs. Wynn, a fifth-grade teacher who just attended a faculty meeting on the school's implementation of a conflict manager plan, thinks the idea behind conflict managers is an excellent one, and she would like to extend the use of conflict managers to her own classroom. She knows that a large amount of time is often devoted to minor behavioral issues that could easily be resolved by conflict managers, while she tackled the major discipline problems. Mrs. Wynn also thinks that conflict management will help students show responsibility, become more independent, and work on their social skills. She feels that allowing all students to participate will encourage students to interact with a more diverse group of students rather than exclusively with the clique to which they may belong; thus, she believes, it will encourage peer relations and tolerance in the classroom. She decides to create a "corner" dedicated to the conflict manager position and to post a sheet describing what conflict managers do and how they are to mediate, along with a sign-up sheet encouraging all students to volunteer for the position. She also plans to have a discussion with her students about this new classroom position to gather their thoughts and feelings on the idea.

When her students return from physical education, Mrs. Wynn discusses conflict managers with them and, after she thinks they understand the position, asks them to take a look at the conflict manager "corner" where she has set up more information regarding the job and a sign-up sheet. Mrs. Wynn informs them that whoever is interested in being a conflict manager can meet with her for a few minutes before and after school in order for her to guide them on learning how to manage and solve problems. Todd, one of Mrs. Wynn's students, thinks this is a great idea and would like to sign up; however, he is hesitant to do so. He wants to be sure that someone from the popular crowd signs up, thus reinforcing that this is a cool thing to do and not something that would be reserved for teacher's pets. While Todd is considering this issue, Jake, one of the popular boys, writes his name on the sign-up sheet. Following Jake, a few other students also sign up and, finally, so does Todd.

Later in the day, Mrs. Wynn decides to take a look at the conflict manager corner and is elated to discover that students have indeed signed up to be conflict managers. "Wonderful! Look at all of the names on the sign-up sheet!" Mrs. Wynn exclaims excitedly as she holds the sign-up sheet with eight names on it. "Conflict managers will be in place tomorrow, and although it will be a learning process for all of us, I will begin delegating minor classroom disputes to them." She adds, "If you signed up to be a conflict manager, please see me after school today or before school tomorrow, so that I can give you some guidance on how to handle the conflicts that may arise."

The following day, after Mrs. Wynn has met with several of her conflict managers and has paired them off in teams of two, she believes they are ready to begin. During group assignments, the first pair of conflict managers have a chance to witness a dispute and to attempt to resolve it. Marsha and Lorna begin arguing over the assignment. "Marsha," Lorna says, "why must you always be the one that writes down the answers to the questions? There are four of us working together; maybe one of us would like to get a chance to write the answers down for a change." Marsha, visibly upset at this accusation, responds, "Lorna, quit being so bossy, no one else has said anything, you are just trying to cause problems because you are such a pain that way." Lorna replies, "Hey! You're the pain; you and your sister are so alike. You just think you are better than all of us because your mom and dad are rich. You think you are so popular, and you are trying to control everything." Marsha blushes and says, looking at the other two students in the group, "I am not the pain, am I? I mean it is always Lorna who is making things difficult; besides, don't you guys think I have better and neater handwriting?" Before the other two students have a chance to respond, Mrs. Wynn interrupts the escalating problem and suggests that the conflict managers try to resolve the problem. Josh and Ava are the conflict manager team that Mrs. Wynn has chosen to resolve this issue.

Mrs. Wynn asks Lorna, Marsha, Josh, and Ava to go to the conflict managers' corner so that they may handle the issue. Josh begins, "OK, here's the situation: each of you will tell your side of the story without interrupting the other person and without name-calling. Once both of you have had a chance to tell your side, Ava and I will proceed with the resolution part of this." As both Lorna and Marsha recount what happened, Josh, Ava, and Mrs. Wynn listen carefully. Once Lorna and Marsha finish with their side of the situation, Ava asks, "OK. Well, Lorna, do you think that there was a different way in which you could have handled this situation?" "No," Lorna replies, and continues, "Marsha is always acting so high and mighty and she does not let anyone else participate." "Well, but couldn't you have asked the group to choose who they all thought should write the answers?" asks Josh.

"You mean like voting?" asks Lorna. "Yes, like voting," replies Ava and continues, "that way it would be more fair." Lorna pauses for a moment and says, "Yeah, I suppose that could be better and that way we would be doing what all of us want, not just Marsha." "OK! I think we have resolved this situation. Right Mrs. Wynn?" asks Josh excitedly. "Well, yes, you have all done a great job; however, I did want to add that there is no need to attack a student personally when the issue is over an assignment. We can just keep the discussion to the task at hand, without any personal attacks," says Mrs. Wynn. The students nod and then they all return to their seats.

Later that day, Mrs. Wynn overhears Jose and Tamika begin a dispute because Tamika chose to be in Ava's group and not in his. "Tamika, we always work together, how come you chose to be in their group?" Jose asks. "Jose, I just want to be in this group. Besides, now that you spend so much time at your father's house, I hardly ever see you. I am constantly at Ava's house and Josh lives just down the street, so I guess I'd rather be in this group," replies Tamika. Jose is visibly upset; he knew that his parents' divorce would affect things, but he did not realize he would lose his friends in the process. Jose quietly returns to his group. Mrs. Wynn, realizing that Jose is upset, approaches Tamika and asks, "Tamika, how do you think what you just said to Jose made him feel?" "I dunno, Mrs. Wynn," Tamika replies and looks toward where Jose is sitting, "I guess bad." "Well, Tamika, tell me how you would feel if Jose had said something similar to you?" Mrs. Wynn asks. Tamika is silent for a moment and then replies, "I guess I may have hurt his feelings because it isn't his fault that his parents got a divorce and he now has to live part of the time with his dad and new stepmom," replies Tamika. "That's right Tamika, thank you for considering the situation. You know, we all have different home environments and many of you have multiple families, so we have to be kind to everyone's feelings." Tamika nods her head in agreement.

DISCUSSION TOPICS

1. *Social Development*

  a. Identify how Mrs. Wynn encourages prosocial behavior. Support your answer with examples from the case.

  b. Illustrate how Mrs. Wynn is helping her students develop their self-esteem. What strategies does she use? Discuss instances that occur in the case study in which a student's self-esteem and/or self-concept may have been affected.

  c. From the perspective of Selman's theory of perspective taking, discuss how this theory may help Mrs. Wynn's students become more mature. Identify strategies that Mrs. Wynn uses to aid her students in perspective taking.

  d. In this case, one of the students is a child of divorce. Discuss how divorce may affect a child's social and emotional development.

  e. Explain how peers and friendship play a role in this case. From the case, can we ascertain students' peer status? Why or why not?

  f. Relate how the different systems of Bronfenbrenner's Ecological Theory are apparent in this case study. Describe how the different systems are influencing social development in this case. Support your answer with examples from the case.

  g. Mrs. Wynn is using conflict managers very similarly to how they are used in the video clip. Discuss some of the advantages of having children take action in conflict resolution. Justify how being a conflict manager may aid in a students' development of social skills.

h. Similar to how the principal, Mrs. Harrington, facilitates in the resolution of a conflict in the video clip, Mrs. Wynn facilitates in her classroom dispute. Share the importance of that facilitation for students' social development.

2. *Erikson's Stages of Psychosocial Development*

    a. Identify which stage of Erikson's stages of psychosocial development the students are likely to be in. Support your answer with examples from the case.

    b. According to Erikson's theory, describe any behaviors illustrating that Mrs. Wynn is aiding her students with the stage "crisis" most associated with this age group. Identify any students who may be experiencing problems with the crisis. Using Erikson's theory, explain how this may have developed.

3. *Bandura's Social Cognitive Theory*

    a. Discuss how Bandura's Social Cognitive Theory is being used in this case. In particular, identify instances that demonstrate observational learning and determine the types of modeling that were employed.

    b. Outline how the use of reinforcers plays a role in this case.

    c. Generate instances where self-efficacy may be evident in the case.

    d. Summarize the importance of Bandura's Social Cognitive Theory in learning situations.

4. *Cognitive Development*

    a. Determine how Piaget's concept of assimilation and/or accommodation is being demonstrated in the case.

b. Identify the stage of Piaget's theory at which most of the students would be functioning. Explain how this stage of cognitive development has implications for reasoning ability and behavior.

c. Evaluate how well Mrs. Wynn is using Vygotsky's concept of scaffolding in the classroom.

d. Outline the importance of understanding a child's cognitive development from Piaget's and Vygotsky's perspectives.

CASE 3

Reaching Out

Suggested Theories/Content: Social Development:
Bronfenbrenner's Ecological Systems Theory,
Parental Divorce

Larry Shockley is a third-grade teacher at Lakewood Elementary School. It is the end of the school day, and he has just stepped into the main administrative office of the school. Mei Lin, the school's guidance counselor, is filing away the last of her students' cumulative records for the day. She looks up as Larry walks in. "Hi, Larry, I am so glad I ran into you. I wanted to talk to you about one of your students." Larry responds, "What a coincidence. I wonder if it is the same student who brings me here. I wanted to talk with you about Alex Hartnett." Mei smiles and extends her hand in the direction of her office. "That's exactly whom I wanted to chat with you about, Larry. If you have a minute, why don't you step into my office?"

Larry begins to discuss some of Alex's classroom behavior with Mei. "These past few days I have noticed Alex engaging in some very disruptive and aggressive behavior. Just yesterday he got into a shouting match with one of my other students. And the day before he outright refused a request by me to return to his seat. This is all such an abrupt change from his behavior a few months ago. I guess now that I think about it, I can see that his behavior has been deteriorating over the past week or so." Mei interrupts Larry by asking, "Larry, how much communication do you have with Alex's parents? I ask because I had a talk with Mrs. Hartnett yesterday, and what I learned during that conversation might help to understand Alex's behavior. You see, Alex's parents recently separated and are looking at a divorce. Mrs. Hartnett was concerned about how Alex was reacting to this conflict at home and was worried that it would carry over to his school behavior." Larry takes a deep breath and responds, "well, that would certainly explain it. I guess the next step is to figure out the best way to approach his behavior in the classroom while remaining sensitive to what he's going through at home. Got any suggestions?"

"Now, hold on just a moment, because the situation becomes even more complex," Mei says. Larry scoots back in his chair and gives her his full attention. She continues, "You see, given the Hartnett's circumstances, Mrs. Hartnett now has to reenter the workforce. She has been a stay-at-home mom since Alex was born. While Alex's parents work through custody and alimony issues, Mrs. Hartnett has already gone ahead and taken a part-time job. This means that Alex is not only experiencing the loss of his father for a good portion of the time, but he now is trying to handle the fact that his mother's time is being devoted to acclimating to a new job." Larry runs his hand through his hair and sighs, "Poor kid, now all of this is starting to fall into place for me. I just couldn't understand how such a good kid could become one of my most disruptive students almost overnight." Mei adds, "Now, I want to take some time to talk with Alex myself. Unfortunately, I see so many students each year as the number of divorces seems to grow higher and higher. Let me talk with Alex and get back with you. For right now, I think you need simply to remain sensitive to what he is going through while still holding him accountable to classroom rules and policies, just as you would for any other student." Larry agrees and promises to review some of the literature about divorce and its effect on children in the classroom.

A few days later, Larry is collecting work from students' desks as they complete an assigned group-work activity. He notices Alex sitting at a table by himself. Larry does one more visual scan of the classroom to ensure there isn't any trouble brewing, then sits down next to Alex. "Hi Alex, why aren't you sitting with your group finishing your work?" Alex shrugs while glancing over at his group. "I don't know; I just don't want to today." Larry notices that Alex has circles under his eyes and seems fairly despondent as he idly doodles on some extra arts and crafts supplies left on the table. Larry asks, "Why not, Alex? You are always such a good student." Alex starts to become visibly upset, "I don't know, Mr. S. Why can't everyone just leave me alone? I just want to be left alone. John and Tyrese were making fun of me because my mom is working at the grocery store now and we had to sell our new car and now drive a piece of junk! Larry tries to think of how to respond to Alex, when Alex surprises him by saying, "It's all my fault because maybe if I was a good kid Dad would have stayed. I always make him so mad because my room is a big mess and I leave my toys all over the house. And it's Mom's fault too. She is always yelling at him whenever he comes home from work. I would leave too if I were him. Who wants to come home and always get yelled at?" Larry puts his hand on Alex's shoulder and gently states, "It's not your fault, Alex. Your parents are working through something they just have to do. But they are going to do the best they can for themselves and you too. I know you must be going through a lot right now. I want you to know you can talk to me if you want. And you can talk to Mrs. Lin too. We are both here for you." "Yeah, I guess." Alex is crying at this point and Larry asks, "Would you like to go talk to Mrs. Lin right now?" Alex nods his head. Larry steps up to the intercom, and a few minutes later Ms. Lin arrives and turns to take Alex to her office. As she reaches the hallway, she turns back to Larry. "I think we are going to have to set up a parent–teacher conference. Understandably, this is very hard on Alex. I think it might be best if we all sit down together and talk about what we can do here at school and at home to help Alex through this." Larry nods his head. "Absolutely, I'll start setting it up."

DISCUSSION TOPICS

1. *Children and Divorce*
   a. Identify some of the reactions children might exhibit in the classroom in response to divorce.
   b. Identify the factors that lead to a good or poor adjustment in divorced families.
   c. Compare and contrast how boys and girls may react to divorce.
   d. Describe how younger children and adolescents might respond to divorce differently.
   e. Extend this discussion by considering how additional demands brought on by Alex's mother's new employment might affect him.

2. *Bronfenbrenner's Ecological Systems Theory*
   a. In the Ecological Systems Theory, different layers of the environment are seen as major influences on the developing person. Can you paraphrase what the microsystem, mesosystem, exosystem, macrosystem, and chronosystem levels refer to?
   b. What levels of Bronfenbrenner's Ecological Systems Theory most apply to this case?
   c. In particular, what level would relate to the proposed parent–teacher conference Mei and Larry are organizing?

3. Parent Involvement

    a. What suggestions might you present to Larry as he prepares to contact Alex's parents?

    b. Evaluate how teachers can best communicate with parents and families as educational partners.

    c. What is the range of parent involvement activities available to parents with restrictive schedules?

4. Student Motivation

    a. What level of Maslow's hierarchy would you say Alex is operating at? How does knowledge of students' need levels help teachers motivate students academically?

    b. Develop some ideas for how teachers can extrinsically motivate students to engage in academic activities despite challenging circumstances occurring in the home environment.

    c. Develop some ideas for how teachers can intrinsically motivate students to engage in academic activities despite challenging circumstances occurring in the home environment.

CASE 4

Choices

Suggested Theories/Content: Moral Development, Social Development, Behavioral and Cognitive Approaches, and Motivation

Russell has just begun Genetics in his eight grade advanced biology class. He really has been looking forward to getting to the genetics section because he has heard from older students that Mr. Willow really makes it fun. After the first section on mapping chromosomes, Russell begins to feel lost. He is not catching on to Mr. Willow's explanations as well as he thought he would. After Russell takes the first test, he gets a 72 percent. Russell is stunned; after all, that is the lowest he has ever scored on a science test.

When Russell gets home his father asks him about the test, and when he hears Russell's score he is not pleased. His father says, "You know, Russell, this is how your sister got started down the path she is on today. First, she failed a test, then it was a major project, soon it was the class, and pretty soon she didn't think she could catch up anymore. So she gave up and quit school. Is this how you want to end up?" Russell stammers, "No, but . . ." "But what?" his father interrupts. "I tell you, Russell, I am not accepting any of this nonsense from you. You bring up that grade or else you will have to quit getting involved in all of these extracurricular things. I told your mother I thought you should be spending more time studying and less time doing other things. Maybe now your mother will stop being so soft and understand that her spoiling you is getting nowhere. I want to see that grade go up, you hear?" his dad asks. "Yes, I hear," Russell answers with a sigh.

His next genetics assignment is a project that counts for 40 percent of his grade, so Russell knows he must do well if he is to raise his grade. After class, he overhears some of the other students commenting on Mr. Willow's class. They all seem to agree that he is really tough, and that this assignment is going to be difficult. Russell was sure that if he tried he could improve his score. After all, science has always been a subject he has excelled in. However, now that he has heard how difficult the assignment is, and having already scored poorly on the test, he's not so confident.

After soccer practice that afternoon, Luis, a senior guard and the star of the team, says to Russell, "I heard you have old man Willow for science. Have you gotten to genetics yet?" "Yeah, we just started it," Russell answers. "Oh, man, his first project is so hard, he has you map the genes in your family, and he grades so strict, you are doomed! Just get ready to flunk it!" "Great," mutters Russell, "I am already in trouble at home for not scoring very high on the test. My parents are really going to be mad if I flunk the project too. My dad is talking about me quitting the team, he thinks it is getting in the way of my work." "Oh—that is really bad news. Does your old man know how important you are to the team?" Luis asks. "I don't know," Russell answers, "and I don't think he really cares, to be honest. My parents don't really know how much playing means to me." "Well," Luis says, "you know, my older brother took Willow's class. I could ask him if he still has the assignments—I mean it's not like they have changed or anything, I hear he has given the same stuff for years." "But, wouldn't he remember the assignment and know it isn't mine?" Russell asks. "Nah, he has graded so many of these over the years that there is no way he'd remember it! I'll ask my brother for it tonight and if he still has it, I'll slip the assignment into your locker tomorrow. I know he got an A on it so you should be on easy street," Luis says as he heads toward the locker room. Russell answers, "Well . . . I guess, I mean . . ." "Hey!" Luis interrupts, "if you are a coward, then forget it, just flunk!" "No, no, it's fine, thanks, Luis!" Russell shouts, "Don't mention it!" Luis shouts back.

The following day Russell finds the assignment in his locker and takes it home to look it over. That night, while Russell is in his room working on his homework, his father tells him he has a phone call. "Hello," Russell says picking up the phone. "Hey, man, it's me, Luis. Did you get what I put in your locker?" Luis asks. "Oh, yes," Russell answers, "I was just about to look it over and I think I'll have to make some changes," Russell continues, "I mean I don't want him to think that . . . well that . . ." "You worry too much," Luis interrupts, "quit acting like such a baby, Russ, everyone has done it at some point or another. You don't want to lose your social life do you, man?" Luis asks. "No, that would suck," Russell agrees. "Russell!" his father yells from the hallway outside his bedroom, "you still talking on the phone? This is all going to end soon if you don't start making good grades." "I gotta go—my dad is at it again!" says Russell. "I hear you, talk to you later," Luis answers. "Yeah—later, Luis," Russell answers before hanging up the phone. Later that night Russell remembers his conversation with Luis and his dad's sermons and decides to make a few minor changes so that he can turn in Luis' brother's assignment as his own.

The following week, when Russell walks in to class, he notices that some of his peers are acting funny; they are giggling and looking around the room. Russell is really puzzled by what is going on. Larry, who sits next to him, says, "Boy, am I glad I didn't skip class today." "Why is that?" Russell asks. "You didn't hear?" Larry continues, "Old man Willow is out for blood!" "Yeah," says Marissa, "the word is that someone in this class forged a paper or something and he is really mad." "I heard he said he was going to make an example of whoever did this to ensure it would never happen again!" says Heidi.

Before Russell has a chance to respond, Mr. Willow comes in accompanied by Mrs. Goodgen, the assistant principal. Mr. Willow turns on the overhead, and there magnified and copied on to overhead paper is Russell's assignment. Russell is stunned; the class is quiet except for a few students' whispers. "Well," says Mr. Willow, "does anyone recognize this paper?" The class is silent. "This paper," Mr. Willow continues, "was turned in last Thursday in this class with a student's name on it. It was turned in as original work to be graded by me." Mr. Willow pauses. "However, this paper is not original work. In fact, it had already been turned in three years ago by another student, a student who received a very high grade and who should remain anonymous." There is whispering filling the room. "So I would like the student who committed the offense to stand and acknowledge what he has done and apologize to the class as well as to me before Mrs. Goodgen escorts him out." The students are all very quiet. Russell is shocked and is beginning to feel sick. "Well, well, well, Russell," Mr. Willow says, "I thought you would like the chance to explain why you turned in someone else's project as your own, especially since you obviously thought you were so smart that you would get away with this." Russell begins to speak, but he can't, he can feel his face turning red and he can hear all of his classmates whispering all around him. Russell wishes he could disappear into the desk.

Mr. Willow decides later that day to call Russell's parents in for a conference to discuss the day's events. "Mrs. Goodgen, do you have a minute?" Mr. Willow asks, poking his head into her office after school has let out for the day. "Sure, Mr. Willow, what can I do for you?" Mrs. Goodgen responds. "Well, I have decided to call Russell's parents in for a conference and would like for you to be present," Mr. Willow says. "Sure, let me know when they can come in, and I will be glad to sit in,"

Mrs. Goodgen says. She then asks "Have you decided how you will handle this incident?" "No," Mr. Willow answers, "I am not sure how to handle this just yet, I need time to think this whole thing over."

DISCUSSION TOPICS

1. *Moral Development*

    a. According to Kohlberg's theory of moral development, determine the level and the stage Russell is functioning in.

    b. According to Kohlberg's theory of moral development, at what level and which stage is Mr. Willow functioning in? Support your answer with examples from the case.

    c. According to Piaget's theory of moral development, at what stage is Russell functioning in? Support your answer with examples from the case.

    d. According to Piaget's theory of moral development, at what stage is Mr. Willow functioning in? Support your answer with examples from the case.

    e. At the close of the case, justify how Russell's situation may be best dealt with according to moral development. Imagine that this situation occurred in your classroom; assemble examples of your strategies for handling plagiarism.

2. *Social Development*

    a. According to Baumrind's parenting styles, identify the style of parenting Russell's father is using. Judging from the research on parenting styles, how may they affect a child's behavior?

b. Discuss how peers play a role in this case. Justify how peers affect behavior and its role in social development.

c. Explain how this incident may have impacted Russell's self-esteem and self-concept.

3. *Behavioral and Cognitive Approaches*

a. According to behaviorism, identify a potential classical conditioning situation in this case study.

b. Describe the type of punishment that Mr. Willow is using. Outline the advantages and disadvantages of using punishment in the classroom.

c. Judging from social cognitive theory, how could Russell's behavior be explained? Validate the roles that self-efficacy and vicarious consequences may have played in this case.

4. *Motivation*

a. Describe the types of motivation that are evident in this case. Support your answer with examples from the case.

b. Conclude from the perspective of achievement motivation theory how Russell's behavior could be explained.

c. Relate, according to goal theory, whether Mr. Willow is setting up mastery or a performance orientation in the classroom.

d. Distinguish between the different motivations that were apparent in this case. In general, describe the importance of motivation for academic achievement.

Identity Lost

Suggested Theories/Content: Identity Development, Social Development, Moral Development, and Cognitive Development

The seniors at Jefferson High School are preparing for this year's senior festivities. Alexa, an eleventh grader, is sitting in sixth-period calculus class with Mr. Tran. She should be paying close attention to the discussion since there is a test at the end of the week; however, she is daydreaming. Ever since Quinn, a senior, asked her to the prom, she has not been able to think of much else. After all, not many junior students get to attend the prom, especially with a guy like Quinn, who is very popular. In fact, except for Mandy, who is also dating a senior and is part of Alexa's new crowd of friends, Alexa has not talked much to most of the people she used to be friendly with. She has made so many new friends now that she is dating Quinn that she does not have much time for her old friends. Some of her girlfriends have argued with her about this, but Alexa does not seem bothered by their accusations. In fact, she thinks that, since most of her old friends are juniors like her, she can just hang out with them next year when all the seniors are gone.

Alexa is staying after school today to watch Quinn's soccer practice and has convinced her friend Mandy to stay with her. Alexa's parents are very strict and they would not have allowed her to remain at school just to watch Quinn's practice, so Alexa told her parents that she and Mandy would be helping out with some of the senior festivities. "So Alexa, are we going over to Quinn's house after practice again?" asks Mandy when they are walking toward the soccer field where students are all gathered around. "Yeah, his parents are never around, and when they are they let him do just about anything so we are all going to hang out there for a while," replies Alexa. "Do your parents think that you are going to come to my house afterward?" asks Mandy. "Of course, silly, you know they would absolutely freak out if they knew I was at Quinn's house. Even though my parents know I am taking the contraceptive pill and you know how you can't get pregnant if you are taking the pill, yet they would still freak out!" says Alexa. "Oh, yeah, I mean you are totally protected on the pill!" exclaims Mandy.

The girls continue chatting as they head toward the soccer field, stopping only briefly to wave at Quinn, who is warming up with the rest of the team. "You know, I used to get along so well with my parents, but it seems like now all they do is ask me things like 'What are you going to do with your life? What career are you going to choose? Where are you going to apply to college?' I mean who cares about these things right now? There is plenty of time later to worry about it. Now I just want to find the perfect dress to wear to the prom!" exclaims Alexa excitedly as she thinks about the prom. "Oh, I know what you mean, but at least your parents ask you what you want to do. My parents already have chosen what I will do, I will be the accountant for our family business. They always tell me how since I am good in math, it will be no problem for me to breeze through school and then come back and settle into a house nearby and work with them," says Mandy as she sighs. "Oh yuck!" exclaims Alexa and continues, "Why would you want to be an accountant? That seems boring to me! I want to do something that deals with fashion, or, well, maybe music, or maybe even travel to Europe for a while. I think it would be totally cool to just wander around all those different countries for a while, I hear that is very popular. Tara's brother is a waiter in some restaurant in Spain and he totally has like the perfect life." "Wow, that does sound exciting," Mandy says, "but I will probably be here, working with my parents while you go off and have all these adventures! Just promise me you'll write me so I can live vicariously through you!" Mandy says jokingly and both girls laugh.

Later that week, Alexa and Quinn are sitting on the bleachers after his soccer practice; they are finalizing the plans for the prom. "So are your parents going to be total losers and not let you stay out all night after prom?" asks Quinn. "We discussed it last night—well, as much as you can discuss anything with them since any discussion usually leads to statements like 'As long as you live under my roof, you will abide by my rules,' and they said that my curfew was still midnight regardless of the prom," Alexa replies in a sorrowful voice. "So are you going to want us to just drop you off after prom? I mean that would be totally stupid, but if you can't stay out, then. . ." Alexa interrupts Quinn and quickly replies, "Oh no, I'll stay out and come home the next day. I mean, I know that it is wrong to always lie to them but they give me little choice. So I suppose they will just ground me as usual. But that is better than fighting with them." "All right," says Quinn. Alexa and Quinn sit quietly for a moment both looking toward the soccer field. Alexa remembers that there is a school-sponsored job fair beginning after school today. "Hey, are you going to go to that job fair the school is having?" asks Alexa. "Nah, I already know where I am going to college, and I have looked into different majors," says Quinn as he shrugs and begins to stand up. "Well, are you ready to get something to eat? You know how soccer gives me an appetite!" Quinn exclaims as he helps Alexa off the bleachers. "Anything gives you an appetite!" Alexa says in a teasing manner as they head toward Quinn's car and join the rest of their friends.

The following day, Alexa stops by Mandy's house on the way home from school to see if she wants to go shopping for prom dresses. Mandy's mom answers the door and motions toward the stairs as she tells Alexa to go upstairs where Mandy is using the computer. As Alexa reaches the top of the stairs, she hears strange sounds coming from her friend's bathroom. Alexa is shocked to find Mandy vomiting, although Mandy explains she just ate something that disagreed with her. However, Alexa wonders if her friend is lying because she has noticed that Mandy has lost a considerable amount of weight over the last few months.

The following day at school Alexa sees Mandy standing by the lockers and hurries to catch up with her. "Hey, Mandy, are you sure you are alright?" Alexa asks her friend while they are walking together to fourth period. "Yeah, I am just putting myself on a strict diet so that I can lose some weight. I want to look good for the prom," Mandy explains. "Oh!" Alexa exclaims, although she wonders if she should have her friend seek help because she now reflects on several past occasions when Mandy has eaten large amounts of food and then has excused herself to use the restroom. Alexa wonders if perhaps she should talk to Ms. Day, the school counselor, about Mandy but then again, what if Mandy gets upset with her for telling the school counselor? Alexa decides that Mandy must know what she is doing, so why should she interfere? After all, Mandy is sure to stop her diet after the prom.

Several weeks later, Alexa finds Quinn talking by his locker with some friends. She gently tugs at his shirt and motions for him to follow her. When they reach a safe distance from the other students, Alexa tells Quinn that they need to talk and to meet her after school on the bleachers. When Quinn arrives, Alexa is already sitting on the farthest section of the bleachers, her face appears swollen and her eyes are red. "What's up?" Quinn asks as he approaches Alexa. "Quinn, I don't know how to say this. . ." Alexa stammers. "Well, just say it, what's wrong, what is the matter?" asks Quinn in a worried manner. "I am pregnant, Quinn," Alexa replies softly as she begins to sob.

DISCUSSION TOPICS

1. ***Identity Development***

   a. Discuss the stage of Erikson's stages of psychosocial development that the students in this case are likely to be in. How is that demonstrated in the case? How are they likely to resolve the crisis that occurs at this stage?

   b. Judging from Erikson's stages of development, account for how each student may be developing an identity.

   c. Explain, from Marcia's Identity Development, where each of the students is with respect to identity development. How is that evident in the case?

   d. Describe how each of the classification statuses from Marcia's theory describes how a person's identity forms.

2. ***Social Development***

   a. According to Baumrind's parenting styles, identify the parenting styles that are being displayed in this case.

   b. Illustrate how each of the parents' styles may be affecting the way in which each of these teenagers behaves.

   c. Discuss the role of peers and relationships with regard to this case. In particular, how may peers have affected the eating disorder that Mandy is struggling with?

   d. Relate how Mandy's self-concept and self-esteem may be impacted by struggling with an eating disorder. How could her eating disorder be directly linked to her identity development?

e. Relay the dangers of eating disorders and their prevalence among teenagers. Compile suggestions for how teachers may handle such issues in the classroom.

f. Discuss the issues that surround teen pregnancy that are presented in this case. Describe how becoming pregnant may affect a teen's self-concept and self-esteem.

g. Elaborate on the issues surrounding teen mothers and teenage sexuality.

h. Discuss how the different systems of Bronfenbrenner's Ecological Theory are apparent in this case study.

i. Detail how the different systems in Bronfenbrenner's theory are influencing social development in this case. Support your answer with examples from the case.

3. *Cognitive Development*

a. Determine at which stage of cognitive development the students are likely to be functioning in. Discuss how this is apparent in the case.

b. Explain instances that demonstrate Piaget's concept of assimilation and/or accommodation.

c. Justify how Piaget's concept of adolescent egocentrism is apparent in this case.

d. Outline Piaget's theory of cognitive development, including his stages. Consider how cognitive development plays a role in behavior.

4. *Moral Development*

a. According to Kohlberg's theory of Moral Reasoning, diagram the level and stages that are apparent in this case.

   b. Summarize how Gilligan's theory sheds light on the events presented in this case.

   c. Distinguish among Kohlberg's and Gilligan's views of moral reasoning. Demonstrate the importance of moral reasoning as well as how it may affect behavioral outcomes.

PART II

Individual Differences and Diversity

CASE 6: Quick Learners

Synopsis: A first-grade teacher notices differences in the abilities of two students and discusses their classroom performance as well as their home environments with another colleague, who suggests she seek the advice of the school psychologist.

CASE 7: Multiple Intelligences
Theory Goes to the Rain Forest

Synopsis: Two teachers collaborate to make use of Multiple Intelligences Theory in their classroom instruction. They focus on the use of learning centers. Challenges ensue when some students are comfortable with traditional types of activities and want to be told the answer. Some are unsure how to proceed with collaborative learning. In short, some are reluctant to use other types of intelligences while others jump at the chance. The teachers struggle with the realistic and appropriate use of Gardner's theory.

 VIDEO CLIP 3: Multiple Intelligences in the Classroom

Video Synopsis: Two teachers work together to create a lesson around Gardner's Theory of Multiple Intelligences.

They employ centers, notebooks, and other devices to manage the activity.

CASE 8: Home and School Cultures

Synopsis: An experienced teacher implements a student research assignment that utilizes instructional technology to facilitate his students' reading achievement, particularly that of his bilingual students whose primary language is not English. He soon encounters some of the teaching hurdles associated with having a diverse student population, including obstacles to parent involvement.

 VIDEO CLIP 6: Teaching in Bilingual Classrooms

Video Synopsis: Teaching in a bilingual classroom poses a unique challenge to a teacher. This clip demonstrates some classroom management techniques that one teacher uses in her classroom.

 VIDEO CLIP 12: Managing Technology in the Classroom

Video Synopsis: The value of technology in the classroom is related directly to how it supports the curriculum. This clip focuses on how technology is used to complete a research project in the intermediate grades.

CASE 9: Teaching Jack and Jill

Synopsis: A teacher struggles with inequitable performance among females in science class. But after talking with other teachers she questions whether there are inherent biases for males and females across subject disciplines. Insight is offered into development of gender roles, including parental and peer influence. The case ends with the teacher considering ways to engage in equitable teaching practices.

CASE 10: Sink or Swim?

Synopsis: A new middle school teacher is faced with being inducted into the ESE referral process when she suspects that one of her students might have a learning disability. The teacher is also challenged as she attempts to adapt her instruction to one student already identified with ADHD. Issues concerning communication with parents, adapting assessment, and classroom management are also apparent.

 VIDEO CLIP 4: Adaptations in the Inclusive Classroom

Video Synopsis: Teachers discuss how they make adaptations that allow special needs students to participate academically within the regular education classroom.

Quick Learners

Suggested Theories/Content: Intelligence: IQ, Origins, Heredity versus Environment, Gifted and Instruction, Parent Involvement

Ann Marie, a first grader in Mrs. Burton's class at Eisenhower Elementary School, is seated at the assisted-reading table, which is where Mrs. Burton guides a small group of students through a story by asking a series of questions that promote literacy understanding. This is Ann Marie's first time at the assisted-reading table and, although she has heard other students talk about this activity, and has observed it from afar because she has been involved in other activities, she wonders if she will enjoy it. Brittney, Joseph, and Manuel are also new at assisted reading, for Mrs. Burton chose groups at random, and they are the last group to engage in this activity. Mrs. Burton soon joins the group, explains the activity, asks if there are any questions, and then begins the story. As the assisted reading activity is taking place, Mrs. Burton notices that not only are Ann Marie and Manuel answering all of the questions correctly but they are doing so considerably faster than the other two students in the group. They are also understanding the relationships between words found in the lesson and comprehending the meaning of the exercises at a quicker pace. As the students approach the end of the assisted reading activity, Mrs. Burton is mentally noting that grouping these students as she has done is not beneficial for this lesson, because there are too many challenges with regard to the students' individual progress. She has always known that not all students learn at the same pace, but she is surprised by how quickly Ann Marie and Manuel are grasping the lesson. She wonders if it was the particular story she chose that captured their interest or if it indeed was the composition of the group; she knows that these students all get along well with each other. She also notes that she may need to make changes with regard to the next assisted reading lesson.

The following day, Mrs. Burton begins the spelling lesson by having the students sit in a circle while they practice their spelling words. Mrs. Burton calls out the spelling word and, beginning with the student closest to her, each student calls out the letter that comes next in the word. If you call out the wrong letter then you are out and simply remove yourself from the circle and go back to your assigned seat where you quietly listen to the rest of the lesson. The students that are still in the circle when the lesson ends win a prize. As the lesson begins, all the students are eagerly participating except for Ann Marie. Ann Marie is engaged, but Mrs. Burton thinks she lacks enthusiasm; in fact, she looks rather bored. Yet, Mrs. Burton notices, despite Ann Marie's lack of interest she has yet to miss a letter, even when she is seemingly not paying attention. The lesson finishes with Ann Marie, Manuel, and Demetri as the winners. "Ann Marie, did you enjoy the spelling task?" Mrs. Burton asks. "Yes, Mrs. Burton, it reminds me of how I play duck, duck, goose with my little brother and sister except here we don't get to run. That is the best part—to run and make it to your spot before the other person catches you," Ann Marie replies. "Oh, yes, I see. But here you are also learning your words," Mrs. Burton says. "Um, no, because I already knew the words for this week; my mom and I usually spell harder words at home. I am so good at spelling; I am the best speller ever!" Ann Marie exclaims proudly. "Well, I am so glad that you like to spell and that your mom helps you. What about the assisted reading activity? Did you like that?" Mrs. Burton asks. "Yes, it was fun because I never heard of that book before and it had a funny ending. But you know what would have been even funnier is if you did not see it coming—you know, if it was a surprise," Ann Marie replies. "Really? Why did you not say that during the session?" Mrs. Burton asks. "Well, they are my friends and, um, well, I did not know if they saw it too or not, and so, um, I don't want to be a know-it-all," Ann Marie says with a smile. Mrs. Burton's attention is diverted to another student and then she awards the prizes and the students are directed to get ready for physical education.

The other student whose progress Mrs. Burton is monitoring is Manuel. As the class begins their math lesson, the students are going to be using different geometric forms in helping them identify the attributes of each shape. Mrs. Burton explains the instructions, pairs the students into groups of two, and then the students begin their work. As Mrs. Burton moves around the pairs of students, she observes how Regina, the student paired with Manuel, seems to be the only one in the pair using the manipulatives. In fact, when Mrs. Burton looks at Manuel's paper, he has already answered most of the questions, and at a quick glance, Mrs. Burton confirms that they are all correct. "Manuel, are you using the shapes to answer your questions?" Mrs. Burton asks, taking the student aside. "Yeah," Manuel responds. "Well, I could not help but notice, though, that you have answered questions on the octagon and that shape has not reached this side of the room yet," Mrs. Burton says as she points to where the octagon is and continues, "See, Melissa and Niya are still working with it." Manuel seems embarrassed and quickly asks if he is in trouble for not using the shapes, which Mrs. Burton immediately clarifies by explaining to him that she just wants to know as much as she can about each student and how they are learning the lessons she assigns. Manuel seemed relieved and then tells her that he does not need to use them although he is unsure as to why he does not need them but others do. In fact, Mrs. Burton recalled a similar instance that occurred when the class was using different manipulatives to solve addition and subtraction numbers. Neither Manuel nor Ann Marie seem to need the manipulatives to arrive at the correct responses, although after being teased by one of their classmates, both students handle the shapes. In fact, Manuel once received a verbal reprimand for using them incorrectly after he and another student, Zoe, had used the shapes as building blocks that they would stack and then immediately knock down. During the rest of the week, Mrs. Burton observes several instances where Ann Marie and Manuel are excelling in the class.

On Friday, during a teacher work day, Gladys Burton is busy incorporating new information into her future lessons. Her colleague Kyle, a second-grade teacher, has just stopped by her classroom on his return from lunch. His classroom is located next to Gladys's and, since this is Gladys' first year teaching, has often called on him for assistance with general questions, paperwork, and so forth. He has been very helpful during her adjustment period. "So, Gladys, how are your students treating you?" Kyle asks in a friendly tone. "Well, things have been going great, they respond very well to my lessons, are excited about getting to work and for the most part are all completing all of their assignments. However, I do have two students that I have been thinking about often. They are completing work faster than I can assign it and I sometimes feel like I may not be challenging them," Gladys responds. "Is it possible that these students you are referring to may be gifted? Do they have test scores in their files?" Kyle asks. "I do not recall seeing any. But that would certainly explain many of the behaviors I am observing! I really did not think that they would be identified so young!" Gladys exclaims and continues, "There is a big difference in their home lives, though, that I have noted; one student's family seems to be very supportive of her education while the other student's family is almost the opposite," Gladys says.

"Really? How so?" asks Kyle, listening attentively. "Well, for example, the class had projects to involve their families in helping them decorate a picture I gave them after having reading one of our books. Ann Marie's family created a wonderful picture with many different materials and colors. Ann Marie told me how her mom had made a trip to the local craft store with her to allow her to choose the items she would use to decorate the picture, and the finished product contained work from her entire family, including her two younger siblings. However, the other student, Manuel, did all the work by himself with what he could find around the house because he told me his mom was busy attending to company. His picture was excellent, especially for not having had received any help. He also told me on another occasion that in his household his parents just did not have too much time to devote individually to him because there were four children in total and they believed that one child should not receive more attention than the other—although in my opinion he is clearly the one that they pay the least attention to because he is not outspoken like the others. In fact, on chatting with his mother informally one day, I learned that she would not admit to one of her children's school work being better than the others' for she did not want them to be jealous of one another. She said she knew the others were jealous of Manuel and, in response, she always tried to downplay any attention he received because she did not want jealousy issues. She proceeded to tell me how all the other children like to watch television and are actively engaged in sports and, while Manuel is involved in sports, it is not his passion; he prefers to read and to invent his own games with their own sets of rules. Although Manuel enjoys television, it is rarely the same program that his siblings are watching. She explained that she did not know why he was so different from his siblings because, after all, they are siblings. I get a feeling that Manuel is beginning to be ashamed of his differences in ability and will actively hide them—to be liked and, ultimately, for fear of ridicule. I guess I am looking for ways to help these students in the classroom and perhaps in the process educate their parents, especially Manuel's, on their children's abilities," Gladys says. The two colleagues chat for a few more minutes and then Kyle gives her some further advice as well as recommends that she see the school psychologist, who can give her further information regarding IQ testing and gifted education.

DISCUSSION TOPICS

1. *Intelligence*

   a. Discuss what intelligence means. Address the debate of intelligence being composed of one ability versus many abilities. Compare and contrast fluid versus crystallized intelligence.

   b. Differentiate between Sternberg's Triarchic Theory of Intelligence and Gardner's Theory of Multiple Intelligences. What implications do these intelligence theories pose for the classroom?

   c. How is intelligence most commonly measured? Discuss the origins of IQ. Summarize how IQ scores are distributed in the population. What is the bell-shaped curve with regard to IQ scores? What proportion of students attains average IQ scores? Discuss the IQ scores that are associated with exceptionalities.

   d. In this case, we see examples of how Ann Marie and Manuel differ from other students with regard to classroom performance. What relationship does intelligence have to achievement? What about to schooling?

   e. In the case, Manuel's mother defends her desire that all her children be similar with respect to achievement.

What relationship exists between intelligence and heredity? Intelligence and environment?

f. Compare and contrast within-class ability grouping and between-class ability grouping. What is the Joplin Plan? Which ability grouping could Mrs. Burton begin using in her classroom? Defend your answer with examples from the case study.

g. Outline how individual differences are most often dealt with in secondary education. Discuss potential advantages and disadvantages of this.

h. Assess how parental views of intelligence might affect a child's classroom achievement. How might ethnicity play a role in individual differences and intelligence? How might socioeconomic status?

i. Summarize some of the next steps that Mrs. Burton could take in order to resolve the issue of individual differences that she has been faced with.

2. *Gifted and Gifted Education*

a. In this case study, Ann Marie and Manuel are exhibiting classroom behaviors that seem to be indicative of their intelligence. Describe what it means to be gifted.

b. Generate the characteristics that Ann Marie and Manuel are exhibiting that would be most consistent with being gifted. What other gifted-student characteristics exist that are not demonstrated in this case?

c. Describe the nature–nurture debate as it pertains to the gifted population.

d. Outline teaching strategies for gifted children. Compare and contrast between acceleration and enrichment, with regard to gifted education.

e. Explain examples of modifications that can be infused into regular instruction to account for students who are gifted.

f. Describe how a student who is gifted may also be learning disabled. Discuss what teaching strategies may aid these exceptional students.

g. Relate the challenges that gifted students face cognitively, socially, and behaviorally.

3. *Parent Involvement*

a. Devise suggestions that you would give Isabel for how to handle issues of intelligence with her students' parents.

b. Evaluate how teachers should best communicate with parents and families as educational partners on this issue.

c. Summarize ideas of how parents and teachers can work together to ensure that a child's educational needs are being met.

CASE 7

Multiple Intelligences Theory Goes to the Rain Forest

 VIDEO: Multiple Intelligences in the Classroom located at *mylabschool.com*

Suggested Theories/Content: Gardner's Multiple Intelligences, Emotional Intelligence, and Sternberg's Triarchic Theory of Intelligence

Melinda Corby is a third-grade teacher with considerable teaching experience. Known for being a pioneer in tackling new teaching initiatives, she has begun her new quest of incorporating Howard Gardner's Theory of Multiple Intelligences into her classroom instruction. She has decided on learning centers as the most obvious approach to exposing children to diverse learning opportunities that speak to their unique talents and learning approaches. She is working with Eileen Hamilton, an experienced team-teacher in her school, and after many long, caffeine-infused collaborative sessions, they have come up with diverse learning centers and a logical approach to organizing those centers and are ready to introduce them to their classes.

"Class, I can't tell you how excited I am that we are beginning our new unit on the rain forest," says Mrs. Corby. "Not only am I excited about the rain forest, I am excited about how we are going to get to know the rain forest. This is something new we have never done before and I am sure you are going to be excited as I am." (She waits a moment to allow the momentum of her excitement to show on her students' faces, then continues.) "We are going to be learning about the plants and animal life that make their homes in the rain forest through fun learning center activities. Take a look around the room. See the different stations we have set up with lots of interesting materials? Not only are we going to read about the rain forest in books, but we are going to be able to see, hear, and feel what the rain forest is like!"

Many students begin to shift excitedly in their seats. Some begin to stand up in anticipation of discovering this novel addition to their classroom. But Mrs. Corby and Mrs. Hamilton also notice that some of the students, eyes wide with confusion, begin to look about to see if anyone else is as dismayed as they are. Some give each other "high fives" and move anxiously toward the centers in an attempt to have the first crack at the project. A student named Reginald is immediately interested, "All right! I'm ready, when do we choose?" (Several other students agree with a vigorous shaking of their heads.) "Well, Reginald, that is our first order of business," Mrs. Corby replies.

As the teachers go through the motions of calling students as their names are pulled from a jar, they ask each student to pick up their assigned folder to chart their progress and attendance at each of the learning centers. As students are called, they begin to make their way to a self-selected learning center. Mrs. Corby assures students that names are chosen randomly and everyone will have a chance to pick first at some point. After all students are actively working at a learning center, the teachers move around the classroom, observing students and helping out where necessary. Mrs. Hamilton makes a beeline for one student who was less than pleased about the ideas of learning centers. "Josh, how is it going? I see you chose the visual arts centers." Josh smiles, then returns her questioning look with nothing shy of bewilderment as he waves his hand across the multitude of materials at this particular station. "Well, Mrs. Hamilton, I don't know where to begin! What am I supposed to be doing?" Mrs. Hamilton smiles patiently and replies, "Josh there are so many fun things to look at here. How about these maps of some of the rain forests in South America? Or these charts of some of the endangered species that make their home there? Then there are some neat pictures taken in the rain forests."

Once Josh is on track and engaged with various pictures of monkeys, Mrs. Hamilton makes her way to other students. She stops momentarily near Avery and Leslie, who are enthusiastically making their way through the interpersonal station. They are engaged in the cooperative problem solving worksheet activity. They begin to argue about their answers and seem to be having trouble managing the conflict, so Mrs. Hamilton moves in quickly to provide assistance. "What are you talking about?" Leslie asks as she begins to get frustrated and angry. "I keep telling you this over and over again, you can't put that down as an answer . . ." Avery responds (without waiting for Leslie to finish), "I know, I know! You have said that a thousand times . . ." At this point Mrs. Hamilton interjects, "Why hello, Leslie and Avery, I see you are passionate about this topic. How can I help out here?"

After squelching the conflict, she continues to circulate about the learning stations. She wonders how two students such as Leslie and Avery can do so well on traditional types of testing, and yet struggle with an activity like this one. She watches as Mrs. Corby also circulates in a very animated fashion, clearly enjoying the class activity as she stops to work with one student who is thoroughly absorbed in his work at the intrapersonal station. Mrs. Corby helps him finish his goal-setting sheet to chart his learning and begin to fill out the checklist of his personal interest inventory in aspects of the rain forest. Mrs. Corby finishes guiding the student, makes her way to Mrs. Hamilton, and exclaims, "I can't believe how well this is going! I just finished working with Chen at the intrapersonal center and he is getting so much out of it! Talk about emotional intelligence! I also can't get over another group's progress in the naturalist station. This topic is ripe for building that intelligence! These are going to be such well-rounded students! I can't wait to make more lessons into learning stations! I have great ideas for upcoming lessons in mathematics, social science, and language arts. I am so excited I can barely stand still!" Mrs. Hamilton hesitates before responding, "OK, I agree, it is going well. Although, I don't know whether you visited some of the groups I observed. It isn't all fun and games; some students are actually struggling. But don't get me wrong . . . I think we are onto something here. We just have to find the way to use this method most effectively."

As the two teachers talk, Mrs. Corby keeps her eyes on the class and notices another group of students clapping their hands in the wonderment of a learning breakthrough. She excuses herself to rush over and congratulate them on their progress. At the same time, Mrs. Hamilton notices that the problem between Leslie and Avery is beginning to escalate. While she makes her way back to the pair, she makes a mental note to return to the issues she and Mrs. Corby had begun to discuss. Clearly there are challenges to teaching through multiple intelligences theory, but then again, she couldn't deny the rewards. She wonders, however, how much should be taught in such a fashion.

DISCUSSION TOPICS

1. Gardner's Theory of Multiple Intelligences

 a. What types of intelligence do you see identified in this case?

 b. Invent other ways these teachers might have conducted the lessons using Howard Gardner's Theory of Multiple Intelligences.

 c. Point out myths or inappropriate uses of Gardner's theory. For instance, distinguish between Gardner's types of intelligence and that of learning styles.

d. Do you think these teachers have adopted a realistic and appropriate use of Gardner's theory in the classroom? Discuss the myth that teachers should try to teach through each of the eight types of intelligence.

e. Can you evaluate your own intelligence profile according to Gardner? What intelligence types are you the strongest?

2. *Emotional Intelligence*

a. What are symptoms of low emotional intelligence?

b. Describe the nature of emotional intelligence in the interchange between Avery and Leslie. How might the teachers have bolstered students' abilities in emotional intelligence to optimize such learning situations? Should this be something teachers do?

c. Compare and contrast the concept of emotional intelligence with elements of Gardner's and Sternberg's theories.

3. *Sternberg's Triarchic Theory of Intelligence*

a. What are the elements to Sternberg's Triarchic Theory of Intelligence?

b. Which types of intelligence do you see evidence of in this case?

c. Ascertain how students scoring lower on traditional testing might perform more strongly using other types of intelligence.

d. Contrast this view of intelligence from that of Gardner.

e. Discuss how an understanding of this view of intelligence aids teachers' classroom decision making.

4. *Intelligence*

a. What relationship does intelligence have to achievement? What about to schooling?

b. How does the notion of a self-fulfilling prophecy relate to intelligence testing?

c. Discuss whether intelligence is best viewed as a general or domain-specific factor.

d. Evaluate whether conventional tests of intelligence are biased. Can we develop culture-fair intelligence tests? Are there ethnic differences in intelligence?

e. Judge how we might use information from intelligence tests most appropriately. How should we view individual and group testing scores differently?

CASE 8

Home and School Cultures

 VIDEO: Teaching in Bilingual Classrooms located at mylabschool.com

 VIDEO: Managing Technology in the Classroom located at mylabschool.com

Suggested Theories/Content: Diversity, Multicultural Education, Bilingualism

Miles Carter is in his fifth year of teaching at Marathon Elementary School, which has a Spanish-speaking student demographic that is higher than in other districts in the state. He has been revising his curriculum out of concern for the grades of some of his ESOL (English for Speakers of Other Languages) students whose primary language is Spanish. He has decided to infuse technology into his reading instruction that will allow for individualized pacing, visual organizers, and opportunities to emphasize key vocabulary words. He knows students really become engaged with the media-rich environment provided by the Internet and educational software, and he sees technology as fun and exciting for all students and thereby an effective strategy for enhancing all students' learning.

As the last students take their seats at the beginning of the day, Mr. Carter begins to outline changes to their reading unit to allow for the technology component he has been organizing the past two nights. "OK, class, I think you are going to like this new change to our reading unit. All of you are going to have a chance to use the computers for this week's unit on Careers and Occupations. You will have a chance to read stories about people with different jobs, complete with pictures, and be able to click on words you don't understand for definitions. We are going to be working in pairs so that if one of you is having trouble, the other can help out! Then, some of your homework will also be based on reading assignments listed on the Web that we will talk about later on." There seems to be a mixed reaction on the part of the students. One student, Reggie, asks, "Well, what about those of us who do not have a computer, Mr. Carter? How are we supposed to get the work done?" His classmate Michael replies, "Reggie, you should come to my house. We always hang out after school anyway. Maybe we could just do our assignments together. Hey, Mr. Carter, is that all right? Can we do our work together if someone else doesn't have a computer?" Mr. Carter replies, "Well, class, that will be OK, but I plan on having some time set aside in class to use the computers here. I want to make sure we each have time to work on the Internet. And as it happens, each of you will be working in pairs since we only have the two computers in our classroom."

He has already sent the first two pairs of students to the two computers in the back of the classroom. He moves the remainder of the class into their cooperative learning groups. They are working on a Jigsaw cooperative learning exercise where each group member is working in their "expert meetings" on a career interest selected from the teacher-prepared materials. They have returned to their original heterogeneous groups, in terms of ethnicity and gender, to share their findings when Miles notices one group is experiencing "trouble in paradise." There is a disagreement among the students over the profession of being a farmer. Rhonda is arguing with Maria, "Farmers don't make any money! Why would anyone want to be a farmer?" Mr. Carter notes the hurt expression on Maria's face, who he assumes has taken the comment to heart, given her migrant family background, and he instantly steps in to reprimand Rhonda for not respecting Maria's feelings. He makes a point to later conclude the large-group discussion with the importance of valuing the merits of diverse occupations and how each has a role to fulfill in society.

He doesn't get very far circling among the groups before one of the students at the computer demands his attention. "Mr. Carter, Ronald is not sharing the computer. Tell him he needs to share. And besides, he is not going to the right websites! I am never going to get my turn if he is not even doing what he is supposed to," Carolyn complains loudly from the back of the room. Mr. Carter immediately makes his way back to the groups at the computer. After he is sure that Ronald and Carolyn are back on track, he stops by the other pair working at the computer. Miguel, who is one of his ESOL students, is in the process of asking Sara what the author means by a portion of the text. Mr. Carter smiles as he watches Miguel and Sara click on the link that will provide clarification and Sara share her own experience in reference to the reading, which seems to shed light on the matter for Miguel.

It is the end of the week and Miles Carter sits at his desk pondering the response he has received to invitations his students have sent, asking parents to come in on the culminating Career Day to share their careers with the class. At this time, Miss Case, who teaches down the hall, walks by his class, "Hard at work as usual, huh, Miles? Always raising the bar for the rest of us!" Mr. Carter smiles sheepishly, "Well, I find it best to try and stay one step ahead of these students! Never let them see you sweat, right?" They talk conversationally as they make their way to the department meeting that will finish off the school day. Mr. Carter decides to share his most recent teaching problem with his colleague. Miss Case summarizes their discussion. "So, you were using this 'Career Day' as an opportunity to close the unit with an appreciation for diverse occupations, but you haven't received the diverse turnout of parents you were hoping for?" Mr. Carter nods in agreement, "Exactly, and when I do get hold of their parents and try to get them involved in the school or the classroom, I get the distinct impression it is about more than just work schedules. It's as if they feel it isn't their place to be involved in school." Miss Case considers that a moment and asks, "Are you sure they don't want to get involved? Some families from different cultural backgrounds may not feel confident coming into the school and participating. You shouldn't automatically assume they don't want to be involved. You should try finding some way for them to be involved in helping their children in the home environment." Mr. Carter sighs and runs his hand across the top of his head before responding, "I have never felt very confident about my own abilities to reach parents. Sure, we all had some exposure to parental involvement in our teacher preparation programs, but I guess I am just not up-to-date on the myriad ways parents might be involved in their children's education and particularly how different cultures might view their roles in their children's education . . . I guess I have a bit of homework myself!"

DISCUSSION TOPICS

1. *Multicultural Education*

   a. What is multicultural education? How can teaching be more "culturally relevant"?

   b. What is the relationship between SES (socioeconomic status) and achievement? In what ways are children from impoverished backgrounds likely to have difficulty in school?

   c. In what ways has the use of the Jigsaw cooperative learning model been shown to be advantageous in creating culturally compatible classrooms? What are other ways teachers can improve relationships among children from different ethnic groups?

    d. What learning styles/preferences have been uncovered that might apply to the Hispanic students in Mr. Carter's classroom? Applying this information, how effective do you think Mr. Carter's instruction will be with these students? What are the caveats to applying such learning styles research to cultural groups uniformly?

    e. Compare and contrast how your own experiences with people of diverse ethnic groups have been similar to or different from what you have heard or previously believed about those groups.

    f. How would you evaluate Mr. Carter's responsiveness to cultural diversity? What suggestions would you make?

2. *Bilingualism*

    a. Multimedia and other technologies are enhancing opportunities for bilingual students and LEP (Limited English Proficient) students. What such technology tools you are familiar with? Evaluate the way Mr. Carter is currently using technology in his reading instruction.

    b. Construct some strategies for scaffolding of reading concepts for students as they master the English language.

    c. Synthesizing across the literature on effective teaching for students in bilingual and ESOL classrooms, what strategies do you think would be effective in Mr. Carter's teaching repertoire? What is he currently doing that is effective? What could be done more effectively?

3. *Parent Involvement*

    a. Identify the range of types of parent involvement the teacher in this case might become familiar with as he attempts to encourage parent involvement across diverse family makeups.

b. Some parents might not see it as their role to be in-volved. How would you empower them to become in-terested in being involved?

c. Analyze how differing cultures of the home and school may conflict as educators seek to encourage parents' involvement in their children's education.

d. Create a website for your own classroom. What in-formation do you feel would be important to provide on such a resource for parents and students?

e. Should teachers encourage parent/family involve-ment? Discuss the advantages from multiple perspec-tives. What do you see as the main challenges to higher rates of parent involvement in the schools?

4. *Educational Technology*

a. How can educational technology be utilized in real-world or problem-based learning?

b. Summarize the hurdles or obstacles that Mr. Carter seems to have encountered in using educational tech-nology in the classroom.

c. Examine how the increased use of educational tech-nology may widen the learning gap between rich and poor students. What about among students of vary-ing gender and ethnic background? What are recom-mendations for reducing inequity in computer access and use?

d. Explain why teachers often do not feel comfortable with computer technology in their classrooms. How can teacher preparation and staff development facili-tate teachers' efficacy in using educational technol-ogy? Evaluate how good you are at using technology. How positive are your attitudes about using educa-tional technology?

Teaching Jack and Jill

Suggested Theories/Content: Gender Roles: Gender Differences and Stereotypes; Socialization of Gender Roles; and Equitable Teaching Practices

Rita Jackson is in her second year of teaching life science at Culbertson High School. As she finalizes her materials for her tenth-grade class, the last few students are entering the classroom and taking their seats. As the bell rings, the class settles down to the business of learning and most turn their attention to Ms. Jackson to see what the day has in store for them. "Class, I am very concerned about some students' scores on the past two science unit tests. I wanted to talk with you about this and see if you might tell me what is going wrong here." A student named Elijah immediately becomes upset, "Ms. Jackson, my parents are going to be real upset if I bring home a bad grade. I just cannot deal with this. I have my soccer playoffs this weekend! Are you sure we all did bad? How did I do?" "Now, Elijah," Ms. Jackson replies, "I don't want all of you to be upset. And I understand you have said you have spent time studying . . . how about the rest of you? Did you spend time going over the reading assignments and lab activities before our test last week?"

Many students begin to shift uneasily in their seats while others refuse to make eye contact with the teacher. A few students are apparently uninterested in the proceedings and a few girls begin to talk among themselves in the back of the room. Ms. Jackson tries to draw their attention back to the class, "Maria and Lydia, would you care to share with the rest of the class? Do you have thoughts on the class's performance?" Lydia mumbles something under her breath while Maria looks decidedly uncomfortable. Lydia decides to make her case, "Well, Ms. Jackson, I don't know about the rest of the class, but I think the tests are really hard. It takes me forever to get through reading all this stuff, and then I still have to make time to sit down and answer all these questions you give us." Many students agree with this point. After Ms. Jackson manages to settle the class back down, she acknowledges Lydia's comment. "I understand what you are saying, Lydia, but I really don't think your homework and study exercises are unrealistically long." "It is more than the amount of work, Ms. Jackson," Maria hesitantly offers, "I didn't even get enough time with the microscope last week when we were discussing plant and animal cells." (Maria looks around shyly to see how others have reacted to her statement.) Ms. Jackson becomes concerned and addresses the class as a whole, "Is there anybody else who felt they didn't get enough time with the equipment?" She watches a few hands hesitantly go up and makes a mental note that many are female students. Ms. Jackson makes a few repeated attempts to question students, but they seem unable or unwilling to offer much insight into their difficulty on the tests. So, at this point she decides it would be better to move on to the first assignment for the day. "OK, class, I will think on this matter and get back to you about it. So, let's move on to today's activity. Today's assignment is something new. Last night I put each of you into groups. You will see the groupings listed on the handout on your desk. You will be estimating the kinds of plant and animal life native to your assigned habitat. You will see there are various materials along the countertops that will aid you in this assignment, so be sure to share with your peers."

Rita waits to see that students are moving efficiently into their groups. As she observes, she notices that Pat Southland, one of her parent aides, has arrived to help out. She takes a moment to greet Pat as she comes up to say hello. "Hi, Rita, look at these kids! This is what school is all about. . . . look at them go right to the business of learning! You sure work wonders with them." Ms. Jackson smiles at the compliment but replies, "Pat, although I surely appreciate the vote of confidence, I am really concerned with their science grades last week, particularly the girls. You remember I told you I was concerned about some of the grades from the previous week? But look at the whole class now. I wish that they were all as excited about all the other aspects of life science!" Pat offers, "Well, I would certainly be glad to help out in anyway I can." "Thanks, Pat, I will probably have to talk to some of the other teachers and see what has worked for them in the past." Ms. Jackson squeezes her hand in thanks as Pat continues, "Sounds like a good plan of attack if I've heard one! Besides, girls are bound to have more trouble with science. I feel so bad for them. When I work with them I make sure to give lots of encouragement for trying and tell them not to take their scores to heart."

At this point there is commotion in the back of the classroom. Elijah has begun teasing a group of girls, to the great amusement of the other guys in his group. Pat acknowledges the disruption, "Well, I guess boys will be boys. I'll circulate and see if I can't help some of the other students." Ms. Jackson excuses herself from Pat and immediately makes her way to the back of the classroom. As she encourages the students to return to their work, she pulls Elijah aside to communicate her disappointment, "Elijah, this isn't the first time I have seen you treating others so unfairly. I just don't understand. You are a good student and you always do so well in my class. Why you choose to behave this way is beyond me." Elijah looks down at his shoes before answering, "I was just kidding around. I have a brother and two sisters and we do that and it's just horsing around. I don't mean anything by it." Ms. Jackson, resigning herself to leaving it for now, responds, "Well, Elijah, I expect more from you. The next time you choose to act this way there will be consequences. Try to treat others as you would want to be treated." At this point, Ms. Jackson makes her way to her desk and is astounded once again at the level of effort she sees going into the habitat activity. If only she could harness that energy for their other science endeavors.

Later that day, Rita Jackson walks to her faculty planning period. She is so engrossed in her predicament she nearly walks right into Tom Davidson as he is making his way to a chair with his cup of coffee. "Oh! I am so sorry, Tom, I wasn't even watching where I was going! I have this problem I am grappling with and nearly didn't see you in time." Tom chuckles and jokingly states, "Sounds like an occupational hazard, Rita. We have all been there before. Care to share such an engrossing problem? I always try to help out a colleague when I can. Car troubles? Love life? It isn't another pesky telemarketing outfit again, is it?" Rita lets out a small laugh, "No, Tom, it is none of those things. I fear I am at my wit's end with my science instruction and some of my female students' performance. I just don't get it, they do well some of the time, but it's just like math! They just struggle with it."

At this point, another faculty member, Miranda Whitman, has made her way to the water cooler and enters the conversation. Tom takes a deep slug of his coffee. "It is true that girls sometimes struggle with science concepts, but I have found that sometimes it is males that are at a disadvantage." Miranda interjects, "Tom, what are you talking about? Everyone knows teachers characteristically spend more time with boys in the math and science areas! And it doesn't even stop there! Take a look at history. Do you have any idea how many hours I have spent trying to come up materials that represent female accomplishments in history? What message are we sending when our female students don't see strong female role models? The curriculum has always been biased in favor of boys! This is exactly why you see single-sex education becoming such a hot topic!" Tom puts up his hands in mock defense, "Well, Miranda, I hear you, and I empathize. But, look at the area of language arts. My male students consistently score more poorly. And I read that from elementary through high school, girls score higher in reading and writing and boys are more frequently in need of remediation in reading." Rita, pauses a moment, then answers with some hesitation, "Why, Tom, I had never considered it that way. Now that I think about it. . . . I have wondered if the fact that most elementary teachers are female poses a problem for boys' identification with their teachers." "Yes," Miranda concedes, "but as long as you bring up language arts, isn't it true that in typical fiction, the titles and lead characters are more often than not males?" Tom replies, "Well the truth is there is certainly evidence of gender bias against both males and females in the classroom. But however interesting this philosophical discussion may be, I see that we are not helping Rita with her problem."

Tom looks at Rita, who by now has her head in her hands in an effort to stem the quickly approaching headache. Rita takes a moment to describe her hours of preparation, orderly lesson presentation, and homework incorporating higher-order questions. She conveys her frustration at her female students' poor performance on the multiple-choice science tests, while noting she has also witnessed that some really seem to enjoy just the social setting of learning as well as the chance to really roll up their sleeves and work with materials hands-on. Tom considers for a moment and then offers, "It sounds as if your students have been trying to tell you what they need. You have learned firsthand that there might be more than one way to approach a learning situation. Couldn't you find some way to use more collaborative activity in your science class?" Miranda replies hopefully, "Yes, Rita, it might be the perfect way to draw in both your male and female students! I think I might even have some professional journals that speak to this issue of aligning female learning styles with more cooperative activities. I am sure they will provide some interesting and practical strategies." At this point, Tom looks inordinately pleased with himself. "Sounds like a good discussion you and Miranda might have over a cup of coffee (as he holds his up proudly and begins to stand up). I have to be going to class now. An old sage's work is never done. More lives to touch and minds to nurture." And he grins.

Rita stares quizzically at Tom's back as he hums a tune on his way out the door. She smiles grimly before saying, "Well, I should have known that my answers would never be solved for me. Where do I start? I fear I am leaving this planning period with more questions than when I walked in! How can I teach in a gender-equitable fashion for both my male and female students? Miranda, would you mind getting together after school?"

DISCUSSION TOPICS

1. *Gender Differences and Stereotypes*

   a. How could Rita Jackson adjust her science instruction to more effectively reach both females and males? Do boys and girls learn differently?

   b. What are typical gender stereotypes evident in this case? What problems are created by gender stereotypes?

   c. Describe what research says about the self-esteem development of boys and girls.

   d. Examine how Pat Southland's comment, "Boys will be boys," might be interpreted in regard to gender role development.

   e. Determine how Maria's tendency to be compliant comes at a cost to her learning.

   f. Assess whether there are gender differences in cognitive abilities.

2. *Socialization of Gender Roles*

a. Where might students like Maria learn that girls are not as able when it comes to the math and science areas?

b. What role does the self-fulfilling prophecy play in perpetuating gender roles?

c. Evaluate how parents, peers, or teachers might be responsible for socializing gender role behavior. What evidence do you see of this in Rita Jackson's classroom?

3. *Equitable Teaching Practices*

a. What is Miranda referring to when she discusses inequitable teaching materials? How can teachers realistically supplement existing curricula materials with more up-to-date materials?

b. Ascertain what evidence of gender bias against either gender exists in this case.

c. How can you avoid sexism in teaching?

d. Suggest alternative ways to measure students' science learning besides traditional and objective pencil-and-paper tests.

e. Debate the pros and cons of single-sex education. Is this really a viable alternative to facilitating both genders' learning?

Sink or Swim?

 VIDEO: Adaptations in the Inclusive Classroom located at *mylabschool.com*

Suggested Theories/Content: Attention Deficit Hyperactivity Disorder (ADHD), Learning Disabilities, and Exceptional Student Education (ESE)

Maria Gonzalez is a new teacher at Newgate Middle School. The school year is beginning and she is looking over the records of her incoming seventh-grade science students. She knows this to be a delicate time in her students' lives as they make the transition from elementary to middle school, and likes to become familiar with her student makeup. As she looks through her records, she notices she has one ESE student, identified as having ADHD. She makes a mental note to later identify key strategies proven to be effective in working with students with this particular challenge, by looking through some of her old teacher-education texts on the subject. She moves on to looking over her lesson plans for the first few weeks of school, making sure all is in order.

It is the first week of her second-period science class, and her students are busily engaged in their cooperative learning groups working on diagrams of the human digestive system. As she is sitting at her desk catching up on some grading, she makes a visual sweep of the classroom. She notices that one group seems to be off task and decides to make her way back there. Randall, her student identified with ADHD, has become physically animated in an exchange with two of his other group members. Ms. Gonzalez queries, "What seems to be the problem, Randall?" Randall takes a deep breath and through gritted teeth mumbles, "I really don't like this project, and they are taking way too long to fill in the chart, so I was just trying to speed things up!" Koko, one of Randall's group members, speaks up, "I'm sorry, Ms. Gonzalez, but Randall is making many careless mistakes on our diagram. And he isn't listening when one of us tries to point them out to him." At this point, Ms. Gonzalez inwardly groans as she realizes she has not gotten to those texts yet to come up with some tips on working with Randall. She smoothes things over with the group by asking everyone to be patient and asking Randall to try and remember that this is a group exercise and everyone must participate to receive credit.

The following day, the class is engaged in a silent seat-work activity. Ms. Gonzalez has set up various learning resources around the room including human digestive charts, models, and texts. When students complete a given worksheet, they are allowed to get up and visit the accompanying learning center. She designed this with Randall in mind, but realizes immediately that it would engage all students. The combination of opportunities to retain information multimodally and opportunities to move about the room would be appreciated by all. She has also set up a conference with Randall's parents later next week in order to discuss strategies that might have been effective in the past with Randall and possibly set up a work-routine journal that Randall can use to set short-term goals in preparation for the longer class assignments that will be forthcoming later in the school year.

During her mental pat on the back, Ms. Gonzalez circles about the classroom and notices that one of her quieter students, Aaliyah, seems to be flustered as she works through the reading passage. She notes that Aaliyah has taken considerably more time to get through the sequence of reading assignments than the rest of the class. She wonders if it is possible that Aaliyah has some sort of learning disability, because she usually responds very well in class, but her performance on certain assignments and quizzes is surprisingly lower than expected. She leans down to the student's desk, "How's it going, Aaliyah? I notice it is taking you a bit longer to get through these reading exercises . . . Can I help in anyway?" Aaliyah sighs and responds in a very dejected fashion, "Not really, I am just not a very good reader. It doesn't really matter what I do, it takes me so much longer than everyone else. I have a real problem with the vocabulary, and I don't even know why I bother trying to get through this stuff. When you explain it in class, I understand so much better. Even the learning centers are more helpful." Ms. Gonzalez smiles in encouragement and points to the nearest learning center, "Why don't you go ahead and visit that learning center for now. We'll talk more about this later." Ms. Gonzalez decides to schedule a visit with Mrs. Goldberg, the ESE specialist, to discuss her concerns. As she checks on Randall, she also notes that while he is not getting into any trouble, he is fidgeting by snapping his pencil repeatedly against his knee and mumbling what appear to be song lyrics, behavior that seems to be only a minor source of distraction to his closest neighbor.

After school that day, Ms. Gonzalez stops by to see Mrs. Goldberg and discuss her concerns about Aaliyah. She shares that while understanding the basics of ESE placement and services, she is so new to teaching that the subtleties of the process elude her. She wants to be sure she helps Aaliyah as much as she can and proceeds to share the symptoms she has identified in Aaliyah that might preclude a learning disability. "Maria, you have done exactly the correct thing. This speaks well of your gut instincts in teaching," Mrs. Goldberg responds with a knowing smile. Maybe it would help if I shared our school's policy in referring students for ESE placement. Have you contacted Aaliyah's parents? That has to be the first step. You also need to check the student's cumulative file. Has she previously qualified for special services or been tested for possible placement? What about her general academic progress as well as within specific subject areas, like math or reading?" Maria is furiously scribbling down Mrs. Goldberg's suggestions and takes a deep breath and blows a few whisps of errant hair out of her eyes before holding up her hands in an all-too-clear sign of information overload. "OK, slow down, I clearly haven't done any of these things and am just at the beginning of this process. I see I have a great deal to learn. And I haven't even had the chance to converse with you about Randall Thompson's Individualized Education Plan (IEP). I have tried a few things, but was hoping to get some more suggestions from you on adapting my instruction to his particular learning needs. I am particularly concerned about my upcoming unit assessment and any accommodations I should make for him. Any chance I can talk you into a cup of coffee on your way home from school?" Mrs. Goldberg checks her watch, considers the obvious potential of this just-out-of-graduate-school teacher, and smiles warmly. "Of course, Maria, I am always available to caring teachers who are clearly willing to learn about all their students, even those with learning challenges. Come on, I know just the place."

DISCUSSION TOPICS

1. ADHD

    a. Identify the typical symptoms associated with ADHD. Which do you notice in Randall's behavior?

    b. Can you create some classroom management strategies that would work for Randall as well as for the class as a whole? What specific cautions would you add that pertain to disciplining students with emotional or behavioral problems?

    c. Identify the common forms of treatment for ADHD.

2. Learning Disabilities

a. Identify the typical symptoms associated with learning disabilities. Which do you notice in Aaliyah's behavior?

b. What role might instructional technology play in teaching students with a learning disability?

c. Present some teaching methods appropriate for students with a learning disability.

d. Evaluate possible testing accommodations that are appropriate for students with a learning disability.

3. Exceptional Student Education (ESE)

a. What are the main requirements that pertain to teaching students with disabilities under the Individuals with Disabilities Education Act (IDEA)?

b. Describe the various types of disabilities and disorders a teacher might be confronted with that are not evidenced in this case. How common are the various disabilities among children in the public schools?

c. Outline the typical process for referring students like Aaliyah to ESE services.

d. Analyze the advantages and problems associated with labeling students.

e. Create a potential Individualized Education Plan (IEP) for Aaliyah.

f. Given the age range you plan to teach, judge which disabilities you feel will pose the greatest challenge for you in your classroom teaching.

4. Parent Involvement

a. Identify parental rights in relation to referring students to ESE services.

b. What suggestions might you present to Maria as she prepares to contact Aaliyah's and Randall's parents?

c. Evaluate how teachers can best communicate with parents and families as educational partners.

d. Analyze why, contrary to popular belief, adolescent students might find the academic transition to middle school particularly difficult.

PART III

Learning Theories

CASE 11: The Note

Synopsis: A middle school student is severely reprimanded by her teacher when her friend passes a note to her. The punishment brings about difficult consequences.

CASE 12: The Shakespearean Dilemma

Synopsis: A teacher who has just relocated to the area decides to present his students with some incentives and rewards when he notices lack of enthusiasm for his traditionally stellar assignment.

CASE 13: The Project

Synopsis: A kindergarten teacher handles various obstacles in her class while instructing her students on respect through the use of modeling and various other techniques.

 VIDEO CLIP 1: Teaching Respect

Video Synopsis: An elementary school teacher has her first graders watch a video to learn the importance of respect and then discusses respect in the classroom.

CASE 14: Mars in Review

Synopsis: A middle school teacher faces issues linked to information-processing capacities and discusses techniques for improving study skills and memory when reviewing a unit on the solar system with his students.

 ### VIDEO CLIP 7: Memory

Video Synopsis: A middle school science teacher encourages student.s to use information in creative ways in order to remember it. As his students attempt to remember the names of bones, they use music as an emotional hook.

CASE 15: A Trip Back in Time

Synopsis: A high school teacher creates a scene from colonial America in order to have her students learn through more authentic approaches to instruction. Students display much enthusiasm and motivation for their collaborative masterpiece.

 ### VIDEO CLIP 9: Motivation

Video Synopsis: A high school teacher uses problem-based learning (PBL) to teach a unit on the local airport. PBL naturally motivates students because they control the project from the beginning and have a stake in its outcome.

CASE 16: Getting Acquainted

Synopsis: A new fifth-grade student experiences the wonders of his first day in a new classroom. Throughout the course of the day, he gets acclimated to his new surroundings with the help of his assigned "helper," who gives him the inside information needed to succeed.

The Note

Suggested Theories/Content: Classical Conditioning, Classroom Management, Behavior Modification, and Social Development

The bell just rang at Pines Middle School indicating that students have five minutes to reach their next class of the day. Students are scattered about, trying to reach their lockers and switch books in time for their next class. "Emily! Hey, wait up," yells Samantha. Emily, pleased to see her best friend coming her way, pauses to allow her friend to catch up to her. "How was Biology?" Samantha asks. "Pretty boring except that Noel swallowed his gum so that Mr. Esques wouldn't give him a detention and ended up choking in the process . . . it was pretty funny!" exclaims Emily. "I bet!" says Samantha and both girls laugh.

As the girls approach their lockers, Jordan, the boy Emily has a crush on, is standing nearby chatting with friends. "Look, Emily, there he is . . . and I think he is looking this way!" says Samantha excitedly. "I doubt it," Emily says as she looks down at her feet and shifts her weight nervously. She then turns her head and quickly opens her locker. As she reaches for her English book, she notices Samantha is no longer standing next to her. In fact, Samantha already had the book she needed for the next class in her bag, so she did not stop by her locker; instead, she walked over to where Jordan was standing and is now talking to him. Emily closes her locker and nervously waits for Samantha to return.

As they walk to class, Samantha tells Emily that she has something to tell her but they reach Mr. Robinson's classroom before they have had a chance to discuss the conversation that Samantha had with Jordan. Mr. Robinson has his students seated in rows that face the front of the class, where his desk is situated. Fearing they will be marked tardy because Mr. Robinson is stern with classroom rules, both girls head toward their assigned seats, with Samantha promising to write Emily a note. The late bell rings and all the students rush to find their seats and begin work on the "problem of the day," a brain teaser that Mr. Robinson writes on the board daily and that students work on while he takes attendance. Emily begins to work on the "problem of the day," although she is having trouble concentrating because she is anxiously awaiting Samantha's note. As Emily finishes her answer to the "problem of the day," she is nudged on the shoulder by Ethan, the student who sits behind her. Emily looks over her shoulder to see a piece of paper folded in four and addressed to her. It must be from Samantha, she thinks to herself and, ensuring that Mr. Robinson is not looking, Emily quickly takes the note and slides it under her answer for the "problem of the day."

Believing that Mr. Robinson is busy taking attendance, Emily opens the note and begins to read it. She is so distracted that she does not realize that Mr. Robinson is walking over to her seat. Emily suddenly hears a noise beside her seat and, much to her dismay, discovers Mr. Robinson standing above her desk. Before she has a chance to put the note away, Mr. Robinson takes it off her desk and heads to the front of the classroom. Emily stares in disbelief. She thinks she hears Samantha in the next row say something, but she is not focusing on anyone but Mr. Robinson. Mr. Robinson reaches his desk and turns to face the class. He then says, "Well, class, I thought that since Emily is so busy working on the problem of the day I would share her answer with the entire class by reading it out loud." Emily is in a panic, and attempts to stop him by saying, "No, Mr. Robinson, that is not my answer, my answer for the problem is right here on my desk." Mr. Robinson does not acknowledge Emily's response and instead begins to read the note out loud to the class.

Emily is very embarrassed, for the note reveals that she has feelings for Jordan, and that she would like to go out on a date with him. Many of the students in the class know Jordan; in fact some of Jordan's basketball teammates are part of the class. Fearing that she will be unable to stop tears from running down her face, Emily runs out of the room and heads toward the girls' bathroom. She is mortified and cannot imagine how she will face her classmates again. After all, right after class, Jordan will surely be informed of what happened and she fears she will not be able to face him either. Emily leaves school before Mr. Robinson's class ends. She phones her mother and asks that she pick her up because she is not feeling well.

Later that night, Samantha phones several times, but Emily does not feel like talking and lets her answering machine take the calls. The following day, Emily awakens when her alarm clock goes off. She begins to get ready for school as usual until she remembers the incident in Mr. Robinson's class. She suddenly begins to feel ill, her stomach begins to hurt, and she feels her body begin to sweat. She tells her parents that she does not feel well and would like to stay home. Since Emily has not missed many school days, her parents agree. However, after Emily claims to be sick the following day, her parents warn that if her condition does not improve she will have to visit the doctor. When Emily returns to school, she decides to skip Mr. Robinson's class. The thought of entering that class makes her feel ill; in fact, just thinking about returning to the class or being in the presence of Mr. Robinson makes Emily feel very ill. She has not returned to Mr. Robinson's class since the incident took place over a week ago and Mr. Robinson has now asked to see her parents.

DISCUSSION TOPICS

1. *Classical Conditioning*

a. Compare classical conditioning to operant conditioning. Distinguish the factors that evidence that classical conditioning is taking place in this case.

b. Diagram the Unconditioned stimulus, the Unconditioned response, the Conditioned stimulus, and the Conditioned response in this case.

c. Explain how the Conditioned response in this case may be extinguished.

d. Decide if a generalization has occurred. Support your answer with examples from the case.

e. Outline how you would ensure that the type of classical conditioning demonstrated in this case does not happen in your classroom.

f. Discuss possible ramifications that this classical conditioning scenario may have in the future. Diagram the benefits that classical conditioning offers for classroom situations.

2. *Behavior Modification*

a. Explain the type of behavior modification that is taking place in this case.

b. Critique how the teacher is using behavior modification in this case. Determine his effectiveness.

c. With regard to the note, generate tactics for how to improve Mr. Robinson's behavior modification. Discuss how you would handle a similar incident in your classroom.

3. *Classroom Management*

a. What type of classroom management strategy does Mr. Robinson demonstrate? Does Mr. Robinson demonstrate "withitness" in the classroom? If so, how? Is he effective?

b. Explain whether you would classify Mr. Robinson's management strategy as a minor or a moderate intervention?

c. With regard to the physical makeup of the classroom, what type of arrangement style does Mr. Robinson have in his classroom? How is that evident in the case?

d. Justify how Mr. Robinson uses the "problem of the day" with regard to classroom management. Judge its effectiveness as a management strategy.

e. Relate the implications that the theory of classical conditioning has on classroom management models.

f. Discuss the importance of a 'nonthreatening environment' and how teachers can provide stimuli that will elicit positive emotional responses.

4. Social Development

a. How may Mr. Robinson's behavior affect Emily's self-esteem? Her self-concept?

b. Discuss how Emily's peers and her friendship with Samantha play a role in her behavior. Summarize the effects of peer relations on teen behaviors.

c. Judging from the case, can you determine Emily's peer status? Why or why not? How could peer status affect Emily's behavior?

The Shakespearean Dilemma

Suggested Theories/Content: Behaviorism, Classroom Management, Motivation, and Cognitive Development

Mr. Malone came into teaching as a second career and taught for several years at a small high school in the Midwest, until his wife's promotion relocated them to a city in the South. Mr. Malone's new job is at a large suburban high school. Mr. Malone has had little trouble adjusting, for he had encountered friendly coworkers and a positive working environment. He has been using most of the lessons that he has taught in the past. He actually was excited to introduce his Shakespeare project because this was always one of the assignments that his previous students had thoroughly enjoyed. The assignment is centered on William Shakespeare's tragedies, comedies, and histories. Each group is assigned a set of plays that they are to analyze, discuss, and then *prepare* for classroom presentations. Mr. Malone allows for creativity in the development of their presentations, suggesting that they use their imaginations for props, costumes, artifacts, and so forth. Students can choose from a range of presentation options such as comparing different scenes, acting out portions of scenes, choosing a theme found in the play and then analyzing how it influences the entire play, and so on. Mr. Malone also has each group create twenty questions. He will choose a few questions from each group to be part of the class's final exam.

He has not heard any complaints; however, he also has not seen much enthusiasm since the project began last week. He wonders if he should have made the last-minute decision to change when the assignment was given from the beginning of the year to later in the year. He wonders whether a large project at the end of the school year may have been a bad idea since students are usually eager for the school year to end and thus may be less motivated to complete such a lengthy task. He is concerned about his students' advancement, judging from the data he has collected via "progress checks." Thus far, Mr. Malone has performed two progress checks, which have yielded poor results. In fact, three out of the five groups are further behind than he had expected and, frankly, he is beginning to worry that they may never catch up. Mr. Malone supposes it was an error on his part to not consider the possibility that the students in his new school would think differently of the assignment.

An example of Mr. Malone's dilemma with the Shakespeare project is group number five, who was assigned *The Merchant of Venice, A Midsummer Night's Dream,* and *The Taming of the Shrew.* The group has four students—Taylor, Nina, Joel, and Eli. Although their classmates have been diligently working on this assignment for the better part of two weeks, this group has barely finished their introductions for each of their plays. Mr. Malone is aware of the problem and is exasperated with them for not getting work done. Last week, Nina earned three detentions for not paying attention, for refusing to return to her seat, and for throwing a pocket mirror at another student. Joel has made it clear to Mr. Malone that he is not interested in English and that he just wants to graduate and, thus, he constantly works on assignments for other teachers in this class and neglects Mr. Malone's assignments. Mr. Malone believes Eli to be a good student but often finds that he is unmotivated and procrastinates until the last possible moment. Taylor, on the other hand, is very assertive and driven and often scores very highly on her assignments; yet she does not seem to be performing at her usual level. Mr. Malone decides to take the weekend to think of some effective techniques that he can introduce to his senior classes that will boost morale regarding the assignment and keep his students' interest on their work.

Mr. Malone greets his students the following Monday and explains that he has added a few things to reward the students who are staying on track. He announces that from now on, he will perform progress checks daily. For every satisfactory progress check earned, students will receive one bonus point toward their project. In addition, he explains, any student who accumulates ten consecutive checks then will also receive a homework pass. The homework pass can be used at any time to replace a homework assignment without penalty. The students seem pleased and most nod their heads and smile at Mr. Malone's new rules. "Wow, Mr. Malone, with all of this talk about work, I have worked up an appetite . . . got anything for that?" asks Vince as the class laughs. "Funny you mention that, Vince, because I actually do have something for that," replies Mr. Malone with a grin. The class is filled with amazement as Mr. Malone continues, "I have noticed that Chichi's pizza is a common hangout for most of you after school and on weekends, so I have worked out a deal with the manager and now have coupons for free pizza slices that I will be awarding to the best three students of the week. These three students must earn satisfactory progress checks for their Shakespeare assignment, they must have turned in all their homework assignments, and they must have no conduct problems—no detentions or calls home." Students are talking among themselves and giving pleased looks to Mr. Malone; a few of them even congratulate him on thinking of involving their favorite hangout. Mr. Malone then asks if there any questions.

Just as he is about to direct the class to begin the day's assignment, Nina asks in a nasty tone, "Do your old stupid rules still apply or are they replaced by these newer and stupider rules?" The class falls silent and most eyes are now on Mr. Malone. "Actually, Nina, your question was a good one in that it brought up the point of new rules and old rules and I will answer by saying that, yes, all of the old rules still apply. It is just that now you have these new ones as well. Your question, though, also demonstrates to the rest of the class how we still are using an old rule: you just earned a detention for disrespectful behavior. In fact, Nina, this is your fourth detention and, thus, you have also demonstrated that four detentions earn you a day of indoor, in-school suspension." Nina shrugs her shoulders and puts her head on her desk. Mr. Malone informs the class that he is posting the new rules on the bulletin board and they will remain there until the end of the year.

Six weeks after the introduction of the new class rules, Mr. Malone's class shows an increase in progress with the Shakespearean project. His students seem to be reacting positively to the bonus points, homework passes, and pizza coupons.

DISCUSSION TOPICS

1. *Behaviorism*

a. From the perspective of operant conditioning, what types of continuous reinforcement is Mr. Malone using?

b. Discuss the role of intermittent reinforcement. How is Mr. Malone using schedules of reinforcement? Is he effective?

c. Illustrate the other types of punishments that Mr. Malone is using. Discuss the role of punishments in a secondary classroom.

d. Evaluate whether you think Mr. Malone is using reinforcement/punishment effectively. If not, how could such reinforcers/punishers be used effectively to manage student behaviors?

e. Devise other Skinnerian behavior modification techniques that are available to teachers in managing their classroom.

f. From the perspective of Behaviorism, summarize the advantages and disadvantages of using applied behavioral analyses as a means for managing behavior in the classroom.

2. Classroom Management

a. What type of classroom management strategy does Mr. Malone demonstrate?

b. Does Mr. Malone demonstrate "withitness" in the classroom? If so, how? Is he effective?

c. Explain how you would classify Mr. Malone's management strategy in terms of a minor or a moderate intervention.

d. Compare different ways to handle aggression in the classroom. Was Mr. Malone's approach with Nina effective.

e. Relate appropriate management methods for this grade level.

3. Motivation

a. Demonstrate how Mr. Malone is using extrinsic motivation in this case. Is he effective in motivating his students?

b. Explain how teachers can help motivate their students.

c. Summarize the importance of increasing intrinsic motivation in the classroom. Explain the methods that Mr. Malone employs in the case study.

4. *Cognitive Development*

a. According to Piaget, determine in which stage these students are functioning. Support your answer using the case.

b. Show how Mr. Malone's knowledge of cognitive development (in particular Piaget's stages) proves helpful in better understanding students.

CASE 13

The Project

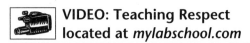 **VIDEO: Teaching Respect**
located at *mylabschool.com*

Suggested Theories/Content: Bandura's Social Cognitive
Theory, Motivation, Memory, and Cognitive Development

M s. Rinaldi's classroom is very colorful, with her students'
work hanging on the bulletin boards. Ms. Rinaldi has
cubbyholes where students place their lunches, book bags,
and so on. Each cubbyhole has the student's name on it,
which Ms. Rinaldi had each student draw so that they each
know which cubbyhole belongs to them. Prior to the students' arrival, Ms. Rinaldi sets up the first activity of the day
by placing all the construction paper in piles arranged by
color on one of the tables closest to her desk. On an adjacent
table, Ms. Rinaldi arranges the crayons and colored pencils,
and on the table closest to the door she places baskets filled
with child-friendly scissors and glue sticks.

 Ms. Rinaldi's kindergarten class—like the children in the
video—watched the movie on being respectful, and Ms. Rinaldi wants to use every chance she gets to remind them of
the movie, thereby reinforcing the movie's message about respect. Ms. Rinaldi's students begin to arrive and they all head
toward their cubbyholes to stow their belongings, then slowly
make their way to their seats. Ms. Rinaldi waits until all the
students are seated, then places her finger over her mouth to
indicate silence. Soon all the students have their fingers over

their lips like Ms. Rinaldi and the room is quiet. "Good morning, it is so nice to see you all today. We have an exciting morning planned so let me tell you what we are going to do," says Ms. Rinaldi. Her students stare at her, some giggling with excitement. She then begins telling them about the activity they will all engage in. She explains that this project is very special for there will be a prize at the end for the student whose work is the best. "A prize!" Paris exclaims excitedly. "Yes, a prize which consists of a surprise for the student who follows my directions and completes their project the best," Ms. Rinaldi says. "It will be me!" shouts Ethan. "No, it's gonna be me silly!" yells Kelly. Ms. Rinaldi quickly says, "OK. I am glad to see that we are all so excited but let's remember that we must respect each other and not call each other names and that we do not call out, we raise our hands first." Ms. Rinaldi sees Amanda put her hand up, and so she answers her question about the project and praises her for raising her hand and waiting until she is called on. Soon, all the students are raising their hands to ask questions and waiting until they are called on.

Ms. Rinaldi proceeds to model the steps that the students must perform in order to complete the project. She demonstrates how they first will color in all the letters they are given by coloring a letter that she has drawn on a large notepad. Then she demonstrates how they will cut each letter and glue the letters on the paper she has given them. She reminds them that the letters have to be in the right order to make a word. She tells the class that whoever has the best project will win the prize. She will grade the project on how well they colored, cut, and glued the letters as well as on the word they made. To help her students remember the steps, she has taped three large cards in the center of each table. The cards have a picture of each step the students must follow: a crayon to remind them to color, scissors to remind them to cut, a glue stick to remind them to glue, and a word to remind them to make a word with their letters. Ms. Rinaldi also has one student model each of the steps so that the other students can watch and ask questions. Once she is sure that all the students understand the project, she tells them they may get started.

Everyone gets up excitedly and rushes to the tables where Ms. Rinaldi has set up the materials. Paris runs to a table, but before she can get her materials, Ms. Rinaldi says, "Paris, remember we don't run in the class, please go back to your seat and then try it again, and be sure to walk this time." Other students who had begun to run quickly stop and slowly walk over to the materials table. As the students get their materials, Ms. Rinaldi says "Marcus, you do not need to get two pairs of scissors, only one of everything per student, please put the other one back." As Marcus puts the extra pair of scissors back on the table, Ms. Rinaldi thanks him for listening. After seeing the incident with Marcus, Cecilia, who had grabbed two glue sticks, quickly puts one back on the table.

Ms. Rinaldi notices that, while most of the students have begun working on the project just as she had demonstrated, some students are not very enthusiastic. When she questions these students, they complain about their inability to complete the project. Paris, one of the students who does not seem happy, mentions that she is bad at cutting and gluing "letters" and asks if she can put the letters in any order because she does not know if she can form a word. Ms. Rinaldi tells Paris to ask herself three questions as she works on each step: Am I coloring in the lines? Am I cutting on the line? Am I gluing in order? She has her repeat these to herself several times. As Paris works on her project, she asks herself: in the lines, on the lines, and in order?

Seated at another table are Ethan, Kelly, Amanda, and Marcus. Marcus is coloring all his letters using only the green crayon when he notices that Kelly is coloring her letters using a variety of colors. Suddenly, Marcus begins to color the rest of his letters in the same colors Kelly has used in hers. Amanda is cutting her letters, careful to cut on the line and not into the letter. "Amanda," Ethan says, "You are so slow, it takes you forever to cut one letter." Amanda stops cutting and replies, "so, I am good at cutting and I like it when it looks nice. Anyway, you are not supposed to call me names, Ms. Rinaldi says it is not nice to say mean things to other kids . . . remember." Ethan lowers his eyes and says, "Sorry." Ms. Rinaldi quickly interjects, "Ethan, I like how you apologized without being told to do so; it seems you learned about hurting each other's feelings . . . just like we discussed after watching the video yesterday." Ethan smiles proudly as Ms. Rinaldi walks away to check on another group's progress.

Ms. Rinaldi sees Roman using the glue on letters prior to cutting them out, so she walks over to him and lightly taps on the card taped to the table, which contains the picture of the scissors to indicate that he has to cut his letters before gluing them. After observing Ms. Rinaldi point to the card, Paris realizes that she, too, has skipped that step, and quickly reaches for the scissors. Ms. Rinaldi exclaims in a loud voice, "Wow look how nicely Shanna has cut her letters, you are really cutting well, Shanna!" Most of the students look over at Shanna and then begin to cut like her. Paris, who is sitting at Shanna's table, compliments Shanna on her cutting as well and Ms. Rinaldi praises Paris' efforts as modeling respect in the classroom.

Ms. Rinaldi announces that they have to begin cleaning up and that all the students need to hand in their projects so she can grade them. Although she had not taught them where to put this particular assignment, the students place their projects on the bin labeled "class work" because this is where many students had put their class projects yesterday and Ms. Rinaldi had praised them for doing so. "OK, class, once you have turned in your projects, I will tell you which student won the prize, "Ms. Rinaldi says. All the students rush to their seats, eagerly waiting to see who is the lucky winner of Ms. Rinaldi's prize.

DISCUSSION TOPICS

1. *Bandura's Social Cognitive Theory*

   a. Discuss how Bandura's Social Cognitive Theory is being used in this case. Determine whether Ms. Rinaldi is effectively using observational learning as part of her teaching strategies. Explain your answer.

   b. Similar to the teacher in the video, Ms. Rinaldi is modeling respect; discuss instances in which this occurs. What type(s) of modeling are used in the case?

   c. The children in the case watch a video on respect. Justify using symbolic models in the classroom and distinguish between live and symbolic models and their effects on behavior.

   d. Explain how reinforcers play a role in this case. Is it consistent with Social Cognitive Theory?

   e. Describe any instances in which self-efficacy may be evident in the case. Summarize the importance of self-efficacy in behavior and achievement.

   f. Justify Ms. Rinaldi's use of self-instructional models (cognitive behavior techniques aimed at teaching individuals to modify their own behavior). Describe an instance in the case.

   g. Explain how self-regulatory learning is being used in this case. Determine its effectiveness.

2. *Motivation*

   a. Identify and discuss the type(s) of motivation being displayed in this case. How does Ms. Rinaldi use motivational strategies in this case? Is she effective in motivating her students?

   b. Distinguish between different motivational models. Generate suggestions for how teachers can motivate students in this age group.

3. *Memory*

   a. Describe how the students' attention is playing a role in their memory. How is Ms. Rinaldi helping her students pay attention?

   b. Determine whether the students are encoding, storing, and retrieving. If so, how is it evident in the case? Which model of human memory is most apparent in this case? Sketch this model and its beliefs with regard to how humans process information.

   c. Present support for the use of long-term memory in this case. Illustrate how an individual's long-term memory is organized. Discuss how teachers can aid in long-term memory storage and retrieval.

   d. Explain how forgetting occurs in this case. Assess how the teacher handles this incident. Generate suggestions for how to diminish forgetting in the classroom. What role do mnemonics play in retrieval and forgetting?

4. *Cognitive Development*

   a. According to Piaget, what stage are these students functioning in? How is that demonstrated in the case?

   b. Conclude whether there are any Piagetian concepts being demonstrated here. How can knowing what cognitive development stage a student is in help the teacher understand that student better?

   c. Explain how Ms. Rinaldi is using Vygotsky's concept of scaffolding in the classroom. Determine her effectiveness and cite examples from the case.

Mars in Review

 VIDEO: Memory
located at *mylabschool.com*

Suggested Theories/Content: Information Processing, Memory, and Operant Conditioning

"Hello there, my favorite sixth graders," Mr. Villanueva says as he greets his students by the door. "How was lunch?" Most students say hello and reply that they enjoyed their lunch time with friends. "As you get settled in to your seats, please notice our lesson for today, which is on the overhead projector." We will be discussing the solar system and some of the properties of each planet. Tyrese, did you bring me back the note I gave you yesterday to take home?" Mr. Villanueva inquires. "Oh, no!" Tyrese cries out and says, "I totally forgot to take it home with me because I left my science folder in my locker! Sorry, Mr. V." "You know, Tyrese, I even reminded you when I saw you in the hall after your seventh period yesterday," Mr. Villanueva says sternly. "I know, Mr. V., and I walked to my locker repeating to myself but then I don't know what happened 'cause I must have forgot," Tyrese says in an apologetic tone. "Well, Tyrese, I am giving you one last chance to return the note to me; otherwise, I am going to have to call your parents," Mr. Villanueva states. "Thanks, Mr. V, I will write it down on my planner again and you know what I'll do . . . I'm gonna move my bracelet from my right hand to my left hand so that it will help me remember, it always works for my mom and dad!" exclaims Tyrese. Mr. Villanueva nods and heads to the front of the class to begin the day's lesson on Pluto, the last planet the class will be studying before their exam on the solar system.

With about half the class time left, Mr. Villanueva begins with a review for their upcoming unit test on the solar system. "OK, class, let's begin reviewing for our test. Remember, for the next two days we will be reviewing so now is the time to ask questions on information that may not be clear to you," Mr. Villanueva says. Most of the students turn their notebooks to a new page to copy down notes. As he begins the review, he walks over to a cardboard cutout that is folded in half and leaning against the side chalkboard and brings it over to display in front of the class. The board is a huge representation of the solar system, with the planets made out of soft foam and, thus, appears in 3-D. "All right, class, remember, this is what our universe looks like—well, of course the real universe is much larger and of course the planets are not made out of foam!" The class laughs. "Of *course* we remember that board, Mr. V! It is so-o-o big and has so much color and stuff on it!" Jackie says pointedly. "Oh, good, so tell me—what is the first planet in our solar system?" Mr. Villanueva asks and nods at Todd, a student in the back who has his hand raised. "Mercury," Todd hesitantly answers. "Yes! Very good, Todd!" Mr. Villanueva exclaims and continues his inquiry, "and so what are the other three inner planets?" Mr. Villanueva nods at Leticia, who has her hand raised. "Um, Venus, Earth and . . ." Leticia answers and hesitates for a moment on the last planet. "It is characteristically known as the red planet," Mr. Villanueva offers. "Oh—it is Mars! I remember because red is my favorite color," Leticia excitedly says. "Yes, Mars is correct Leticia . . . Good job!" Mr. Villanueva exclaims and then asks the class, "What else do we know about Mars?" "That its climate is dry and cold, kind of like it is here," says Matthew and many students laugh. "Right, very good," Mr. Villanueva says, grinning. "Mars has a thin atmosphere," Natalie states. "Yes,"

Mr. Villanueva says and asks, "What is Mars's atmosphere made up of?" "Carbon, um, monoxide, no—I mean carbon dioxide," says Miguel as he blushes. "That is OK, Miguel, it is an easy mistake to make because the two are very close, so I am impressed that you could remember the difference and correct your mistake." Miguel nods and smiles at Mr. Villanueva as he looks down at his desk.

"OK, so what else do we know about Mars?" Mr. Villanueva asks the class. "That every year it has dust storms that affect the whole planet. I remember that because I am allergic to dust," Tyrese says. Natalie replies "Wow, you must sneeze a lot." "Yeah!" Tyrese replies, and many students laugh. "OK. So, how many satellites are there on Mars?" Mr. Villanueva asks the class. "Three?" Jackie answers in the form of a question. "No, not three," Mr. Villanueva says. "Two," replies Teresa. "That is right!" Mr. Villanueva says and continues, "Can anyone remember their names?" "Isn't one called phobia?" asks Matthew. "No, that is a fear of something, you dork!" says Leticia and the class laughs. "Yeah, like living in a place like Mars! Can you imagine?" Natalie asks. "No, because it would be creepy, I mean there is no life on Mars right, Mr. V?" Abby asks. "No, Abby there is no life on Mars today, although there is speculation that at one time the conditions might have allowed for it because runoffs of water were discovered," Mr. Villanueva says and continues, "the name of the satellite is Phobos, so you were close, Matthew—and no name-calling, Leticia." "Sorry, Mr. V," Leticia says. Mr. Villanueva nods at Leticia to acknowledge her apology. "The other satellite is called Deimos, it's the smaller of the two, right, Mr. V?" says Todd. "That is correct!" Mr. Villanueva says. "Great review of Mars, class!" Mr. Villanueva says. "Are there any questions?" Mr. Villanueva asks. "Is Mars the only planet on the test?" asks Jackie. "No Jackie, please remember that the test is on the entire solar system and we will review all the planets before the test," Mr. Villanueva replies. "Yeah, I usually just repeat it over and over again until it just gets into my brain," declares Leticia. "That is good, but also do not forget to remember the new information by adding it to information you already know, like you did earlier, Leticia, with the color red," says Mr. Villanueva. "Oh, yeah," Leticia says. "Do we have to know all of the stuff about each one and also the order they go in? Because I am not that good with that, I always forget the ones in the middle but always remember the ones at the beginning and at the end," Jackie states worriedly. "Yes, you will have to know all the planets and their order and, actually, for tonight's homework, I want you to create a sentence out of the first letter of each of the planets in the solar system order to help with your review. Tomorrow we will share our sentences with each other and I will tell you one that always works for me," states Mr. Villanueva. Matthew replies, "Oh, but Mr. V., tells us yours now." "No, no, I would like to give you the chance to construct your own using your own experiences. Use your imagination and try to picture images in your head that relate to the information you are studying. OK?" replies Mr. Villanueva and Matthew smiles. "Great! There's the bell, class, so you are dismissed!" The students quickly pack up their belongings and head toward the door.

DISCUSSION TOPICS

1. *Information Processing*
   a. Identify examples in this case that depict episodic memory.
   b. Relate examples in this case that depict semantic memory.
   c. Generate examples in this case that depict explicit memory.

2. Memory

a. Explain how Mr. Villanueva captures his students' attention. Discuss the importance of attention in memory and recall.

b. Identify examples in this case of short-term memory use. What limitations exist in short-term/working memory? Discuss at least one limitation demonstrated in this case.

c. How do the students in Mr. Villanueva's class demonstrate the use of long-term memory?

d. Explain rehearsal in long-term memory. Describe an instance in the case in which rehearsal is being employed.

e. How does forming images aid our retrieval of information? Is the use of visual imagery present in this case? Discuss how Mr. Villanueva encourages the use of visual imagery.

f. Discuss what meaningful learning is. How does it differ from rote memorization? Discuss instances in the case of meaningful learning.

g. Elaborations aid our memory; summarize how elaborations are used in this case.

h. What is the advantage of using mnemonics? Identify the type(s) of mnemonics that Mr. Villanueva discusses in the case.

i. Recount how Mr. Villanueva employs retrieval cues in this case. How do retrieval cues aid our recall of information?

j. Explain the serial positioning effect. Which student in the case is showing evidence of having this problem?

k. Mr. Villanueva presents information in an organized manner. How does organization aid our memory?

Generate other types of organization that you could use in the classroom to aid your students' learning and recall of material. Illustrate how the video clip may help you.

3. *Operant Conditioning*

   a. Distinguish between the different types of positive reinforcers used in this case.

   b. Discuss at least two instances in which a positive reinforcer was used and discuss its effectiveness on modifying behavior.

   c. Can you relate instances in which Mr. Villanueva uses punishment? If so, how does he employ it? Is it successful?

   d. Relate how teachers employ reinforcement and punishment effectively. Support your answer.

CASE 15

A Trip Back in Time

 **Video: Motivation
located at *mylabschool.com***

Suggested Theories/Content: Social Constructivism, Motivation, Identity Development, and Cognitive Development

M s. Rixen's sophomore students are very excited as they walk back to their classroom from lunch because today is the day that the Rixen Shoppe opens. They have been anxiously awaiting this day for the past few weeks and they have all been engaged in working toward the Shoppe ever since the concept was introduced to them. Ms. Rixen is known for her unique projects, which allow students to be engaged with different learning approaches and on different levels. Ms. Rixen's students usually score very well on all of her assignments.

"I am so excited for the Shoppe to open," says Lori as she closes her locker. "I know exactly what you mean, it is like all the work we have been doing is finally going to pay off!" replies Natasha. "Hey there! Ready for the Shoppe?" asks Nila as she approaches her two classmates in the hallway. "Oh yeah, we were just talking about it! I am even excited to see what costumes Ms. Rixen came up with!" exclaims Lori. "I know, I just can't believe she is pulling this off. You know, so many people I have talked to are so jealous that we have Ms. Rixen because not many of the other teachers take teaching to this level!" exclaims Natasha. "I know, and the weird thing is, with all this research we had to do, I actually found myself getting into it—I mean my character, you know, is in love with a boy whose family is in a feud with mine. So although we are in love, we cannot marry, and actually, I am promised to marry this man who is, like, thirty years older than me," Nila responds. Lori adds, "I mean can you imagine living in a time in which women were given off in marriage to whomever their father chose? That is totally insane." "Actually," Nila states, "you know the section of the assignment where we had to research how one of our colonial problems could tie into our society today? Well, I learned all about arranged marriages and how there are societies that still practice this today." "Really?" Lori asks. "Where?" "Well, you are going to find out all about it when my group goes on Friday." Nila says and smiles proudly. "Hey, cool," Lori replies.

"Hey, do you all think this lipstick looks good on me?" asks Natasha, examining her lipstick in her locker mirror. Lori and Nila agree that it does. "OK, well, let's go there, lipstick woman, or we are going to be late," Nila adds jokingly as she gently pokes her elbow into her friend's arm. "Yeah, yeah, but let's remember who my colonial husband is; I mean, is he hot or what?" asks Natasha. The girls agree once more and, as they walk to class, Lori says, "You know, I hope Ms. Rixen does not make us take our makeup off—I mean, they did not use it back then." Ms. Rixen overhears her students and decides to interject, "Now ladies, I would not do that. My goal is not to interfere with your social lives, but rather to teach you a thing or two about history." All of them laugh and they enter the classroom.

The Rixen Shoppe is not an actual store but a stagelike theatre in which all the projects and presentations will be taking place while the rest of the students serve as the audience. Ms. Rixen's classroom has been turned into a picturesque scene directly from colonial America. The desks have all been moved to the front of the class and the room has been converted into a storefront and actual store. A sign that reads

"The Rixen Shoppe" in simple black letters is hung on top of the door the students created. On the wall closest to the classroom entrance hangs a bulletin board that explains what the Rixen Shoppe is, what it is for, and which learning units are associated with this assignment. The students are assessed traditionally in the form of unit tests based on the book chapters, but also alternatively in the form of portfolios, summaries, presentation reports, and live presentations. Ms. Rixen has even included peer evaluations as part of their assessments. The audience members all receive a copy of the presentation report that each group has created. On it are the items labeled for evaluation. Peers evaluate those items and turn in their evaluations to Ms. Rixen, who will also assess the presentation report as well as all the other assignments.

The Rixen Shoppe is a concept that all the students have taken part in and have helped construct for the last few weeks. Ms. Rixen wanted to have her students experience real-life situations based on a store in which they could employ the concepts they are learning in the classroom. The Rixen Shoppe is unique in that it represents colonial America. Thus, the store, its visitors, and owners experience colonial America. Every student in the class plays a role in the store because each is assigned to a family or is a single character with real-life problems to resolve that were typical of the times. Ms. Rixen researched problems traditionally encountered in colonial America and created learning situations that students could investigate and resolve according to those times. Ms. Rixen based each of the problems in general domains: Currency, Customs, Education, Medicine, Religion, and Transportation. Each family of students was given two problems to explore and create a portfolio for. A general assignment was also given to the class, which each student was expected to summarize. Students also created out of construction paper, paper, construction foam, and poster board all aspects of the store and their individual portfolios. Ms. Rixen, who was a good seamstress, was also able to construct costumes that resembled the appropriate attire for the times, which she felt would give the students a chance to fully experience an entirely different way of life.

The students are all standing around admiring their work and discussing the Shoppe when the final bell rings indicating that class has begun. "All right, everyone, please listen," says Ms. Rixen loudly. "You are all aware of which days you present, according to my list, the Windsor family presents today along with the Calvert family. Thus, the students belonging to those families as well as the Shoppe owners need to go over to the costume area, find their names, and please put the costumes on. The rest of you, please pick up a grading sheet. Remember, you will provide me with comments and help me assess your classmates on their performances." All the students hurriedly assume their roles and soon the class is transported back in time.

DISCUSSION TOPICS

1. ***Social Constructivism***
   a. Discuss the theory of situated cognition. How does this case support their claims?
   b. Explain problem-based learning and discuss how it is used in this case and in the video.
   c. Discuss authentic instruction and its implications for education. Refer to aspects of this case that depict authentic instruction. In what other ways can teachers employ authentic instruction in the classroom?
   d. Relate examples in this case in which the teacher used cooperative learning. Identify the key aspects of cooperative learning. Discuss how to compose the group and its advantages for instruction.
   e. Establish how scaffolding is taking place in this case. Discuss how teachers can use Vygotsky's theory in the classroom.

   f. Compare and contrast the differences that exist in the planning of an effective authentic assessment situation and a traditional one.

2. Motivation

   a. Explain how Ms. Rixen motivated her students to take part in the class project.

   b. What types of motivation are evident in this case?

   c. According to achievement motivation theory, explain the students' behavior.

   d. According to goal theory, conclude whether Ms. Rixen is setting up mastery or performance orientations in the classroom.

3. Identity Development

   a. Identify which of Erikson's stages of psychosocial development the students are likely to be functioning in. Support your answer using examples from the case.

   b. Describe how this class project may aid Ms. Rixen's students with that stage's crisis.

   c. Diagram how identity is formed and how self-concept is developed.

   d. Appraise Marcia's theory of identity development in relation to this case.

4. Cognitive Development

   a. Which Piagetian stage of cognitive development are these students likely to be in? How is that demonstrated in the case?

   b. Discuss adolescent egocentrism and cite examples from the case.

CASE 16

Getting Acquainted

Suggested Theories/Content: Applications of Operant Conditioning, Classroom Management, Social Development, and Social Cognitive Theory

Carlos is a new student and this is his first day. When he arrives at the school, his mother helps him find Mrs. Sims's class, which is where he has been assigned. The school is large and students are going in all directions to their classes. Some students are talking in groups, while others are standing outside their classrooms by themselves. A group of boys just ran by Carlos and almost knocked him over. Before either he or his mother could react to what had occurred, they heard a male voice yell for the boys to stop running. This was very different from what Carlos was used to; his last school was small and he had grown up with most of the children who attended the school. "Mrs. Sims's fifth-grade class, here we are, Carlos," his mother exclaims as she opens the door.

Carlos and his mom enter the classroom to find some students sitting in their seats, others sitting on their desks casually involved in conversation. The teacher, Mrs. Sims, comes to greet them. "Hi, I am Mrs. Sims," she states, holding out her hand to both Carlos and his mother. "Welcome to my classroom. I am so happy you are joining us." While Mrs. Sims and Carlos's mother speak briefly, Carlos surveys the room. There are many colorful charts and graphs on the walls and bulletin boards with what looks like students' work displayed on them. The desks are arranged in rows but are grouped by twos. There are computers located in the back of the class-room next to a sink area. Just as some of the students begin to take notice of Carlos, the bell sounds and the teacher announces that students need to find their seats. Carlos and his mom say their good-byes, and Mrs. Sims introduces him to the class. She explains to Carlos that for the next few days, his helper will be Lucy. Lucy has already been briefed on her responsibilities and knows that she is to help him in any way she can until he becomes acclimated to the new classroom. Mrs. Sims then motions for Carlos to take a seat next to Lucy, who has her hand raised and is waving for him to come over and sit by her.

"Hi! I am Lucy," she exclaims excitedly. "Your seat will be here." She pats the seat next to her and continues, "We always begin the day with math; we are doing long-division. Open your book to page 56 and do problems 5 through 20. Did you bring paper?" Lucy asks. "Yeah, I brought a backpack with all my stuff," Carlos replies. "OK, oh—you need to go and store your stuff in the cubbyhole area; the names are alphabetized," Lucy says. Carlos nods and heads over to the cubbyhole area to put his things away. As Carlos is heading back to his desk, he notices that students have placed their homework on the edge of their desk and that Mrs. Sims is coming around and checking it off in her grade book. Some students, he notices, are getting little star stickers and they look pleased. He decides that when there is some free time he is going to ask Lucy what the stars mean. After Mrs. Sims finishes checking homework, the students who received stars are allowed to go to a chart beside Mrs. Sims's desk that has all the students' names on it and several places to put stars next to their name.

"Mrs. Sims always walks around the room when the students are working at their seats and you will get into trouble if you are not doing your work," Lucy explains to Carlos. She directs his attention to a board hanging on one of the walls of the class that is labeled "Class Rules" and tells him to learn those because some might be different from the rules at his old school. Carlos agrees and decides to go and take a look as soon as he is finished with his problems. Before Carlos is finished, he sees Mrs. Sims motion to a student to meet her at the front of the class by her desk. Although Carlos still has a few problems to complete, he cannot help but be intrigued by what is happening and thus decides to listen as Mrs. Sims and the student converse. Mrs. Sims says, "Sara, I have repeatedly told you not to look onto your classmate's work, yet you continue to disobey me. We signed the class contract together ensuring that you knew you were breaking class rule number four and what you were going to do so that this behavior would not occur again. Yet, I have caught you looking at a classmate's paper three times this week. As we agreed, you have now lost the chance to earn stars for the next week, and I will remove any stars you earned last week. Sara, obviously upset, replies in a whiney tone, "But, Mrs. Sims, I wasn't looking at his paper, I was just . . ." "Sara," Mrs. Sims interrupts, "I don't want to hear any more on this subject or you are going to increase your punishment and lose recess. Now, please go and sit down and finish your work." Sara looks disappointed but returns to her desk in silence. Mrs. Sims resumes walking around and supervising her students' work. Carlos looks over at Lucy, who seems to not even have noticed Sara being reprimanded for she is busy solving her problems. Carlos decides to do the same and gets back to his work.

"OK, class, please hand your papers to Sophie, who is the classroom helper for today and as I call you, come to the board and work on the problems I have written." Carlos notices three students being called to work on the two long-division problems on the board. Just as the students get started on the board problems, Mrs. Sims walks toward the back of the classroom where two boys are sitting. "Srin and Adam," she sternly asks, "What is that you are passing back and forth to each other?" As the boys stammer an answer, Mrs. Sims takes the paper from one of them and informs them that she had already given them a warning and they ignored it; thus, now they have both lost their recess. The boys look sullen but do not say anything and Mrs. Sims returns to the front of the class.

Mrs. Sims turns her attention to the problems on the board. She checks the first problem which Hing-Su completed, and exclaims, "Excellent work, Hing Su! You have earned a purple star on the star chart!" Mrs. Sims hands Hing-Su a purple star, which she happily places next to her name on the star chart. Carlos seizes this moment to ask Lucy about the stars and their meaning. Lucy explains that the students are very excited when there are opportunities to earn stars because they know there are different consequences for different stars. During lessons, they can earn purple stars to put on the star chart and for every five purple stars they earn they get a chance at Mrs. Sims's grab bag. Carlos has never heard of a grab bag, so Lucy tells him that it is a bag of prizes that Mrs. Sims has decorated and is filled with different school supplies, candy, and small toys. Lucy also tells Carlos that yellow stars can be earned for behavior and for being a class helper, and that you need three of those to get a chance at the grab bag. "Finally," Lucy tells Carlos, "there are stars that you can earn for assignments and homework; these are the silver stars and you never know how many of these stars are needed. Mrs. Sims always changes the number and so it is exciting because you never know when you may get lucky!" Mrs. Sims looks over at Lucy and Carlos and nods her head approvingly.

As Mrs. Sims looks over the second chalkboard problem, she notices that unlike Hing-Su, Ryan, who completed this problem, has made several errors. "Ryan, that was a good try; however, the problem is not correct," states Mrs. Sims and then asks for a volunteer to fix the problem. Teresa raises her hand and Mrs. Sims motions for her to attempt the problem that Ryan was unable to do correctly. Within moments, Teresa has corrected Ryan's mistakes and she too earns a purple star to place on the star chart. This is not the first time that Ryan has demonstrated difficulty with long-division; thus, Mrs. Sims decides to ask Teresa to switch seats with the student sitting next to Ryan so that she may serve as his helper during this lesson. Mrs. Sims employs helpers in the classroom often and finds that this process is well received by students; thus, she has been encouraged to continue the practice.

The lesson continues as Mrs. Sims checks the third problem on the board and finds that the answer is also incorrect. She proceeds to ask for a volunteer to correct the problem and is happy to see that Carlos's hand is raised. She calls on Carlos to come to the board and is pleased to see that her new student solves the problem correctly. "Well, Carlos," Mrs. Sims says, "you have earned your first star, a purple one. Did Lucy explain what they mean? If you have any questions, please feel free to ask me, OK?" Carlos nods and Mrs. Sims continues, "I am very proud of you for volunteering on your first day! Good for you! Here's your star, just place it next to your name on the star chart where it is labeled 'purple stars'." Carlos walks over proudly and places the star next to his name.

DISCUSSION TOPICS

1. *Applications of Operant Conditioning*
    a. How is Mrs. Sims using reinforcers in the classroom? Are they effective in modifying student behavior?
    b. Distinguish between the different type of reinforcers. Which are being demonstrated in this case?
    c. Compare and contrast intermittent schedules of reinforcement. Conclude how they differ from continuous reinforcement.
    d. Diagram the different schedules of reinforcement being used in this case.
    e. Explain the purpose of a contingency contract. Does Mrs. Sims use contracts? If so, is their use in her class proving effective?
    f. Interpret the implications that the theory of operant conditioning may have on behavior modification.

2. Classroom Management

a. Identify the type of classroom management strategy that Mrs. Sims demonstrates.

b. Conclude whether Mrs. Sims demonstrates "withitness" in the classroom. If so, support your answer with examples from the case and explain her level of effectiveness.

c. Show, using examples in the case, how Mrs. Sims uses the problems from the book that all students begin the day with as a classroom management technique.

3. Social Development

a. Support the notion that being a class helper aids in the development of self-esteem and self-concept.

b. In the case, Mrs. Sims demonstrates the use of prosocial behaviors in the classroom. Devise other tactics that can aid teachers in promoting prosocial behaviors in the classroom.

4. Social Cognitive Theory

a. Describe how vicarious reinforcement and punishment might be playing a role in this case.

b. Determine whether Mrs. Sims is using observational learning in this case. Should you conclude that she is not, design methods for how Mrs. Sims could use observational learning in her class. Generate other techniques that could apply to other classroom situations.

c. Outline how Bandura's social cognitive theory is being used in this case. Specifically, diagram how modeling and peer tutoring are being used.

d. Synthesize across the research on Bandura's concept of modeling and peer modeling/tutoring. Summarize its advantages for classroom use.

CASE 17: Backfired

Synopsis: Carl Little is a first-year teacher at Bernadette Elementary School. Bernadette is a small school located in a predominantly urban school district. Mr. Little has been motivated from the start to provide the best atmosphere possible to his fifth-grade students. He recently graduated from the local college with his degree in elementary education. One lesson that really made an impression on him during his training was the practice of using extrinsic rewards to increase students' desirable behavior.

CASE 18: Giving Up

Synopsis: A middle school teacher experiences the challenge of motivating a student who has given up in the face of failure. After a few initial attempts, the teacher realizes it is going to take a systematic plan of action in order to help this student over the immense hurdle of repeated failure.

CASE 19: To Belong or Not to Belong

Synopsis: A teacher struggles with clique-like behavior, challenges particular to the high school transition, students' developmental changes, and the misplaced motivation of students in his tenth-grade literature class. The case ends with the teacher contemplating cooperative learning and community and family involvement as possible solutions.

CASE 17

Backfired

Suggested Theories/Content: Extrinsic and Intrinsic Motivation and Goal Orientations

Carl Little has instructed his class from the very start that those who score a 90 percent on the multiple-choice unit tests would each earn a no-homework pass. Mr. Little felt this reinforcer would work with all students. Students were genuinely excited, and the rewards had been quite effective so far in motivating students to really apply themselves in class. It is now the second month of the school year, and Mr. Little is about to introduce the lesson on world continents. He waits for the students as they begin to settle down and turn their attention to the front of the class. He smiles and then begins, "OK, class, now that I have your attention I'd like to introduce our next unit, titled 'World Continents.' I am sure you are going to enjoy this topic. World geography has always been one of my favorite areas of study. So, if you will now turn to page . . ." Interrupting the teacher, a student named Rachel exclaims, "Wait a minute, Mr. Little! Why do we have to learn about places halfway across the world? I don't care about places I am never gonna get to see. What's the point?" Mr. Little looks pointedly at the student and responds, "Rachel, I don't like to discourage student questions, but you know what our class rule is on talking out of turn. You have to raise your hand first. Besides, this is a very important lesson. There will be an important test at the end of the week on this material. So, I suggest we get to work."

Later the same day, Mr. Little has just concluded the opening lesson on Asia. A student named Jesse shares his interest. "Wow, Mr. Little, that was really cool! When do we hear about Europe? That's where all those kings and queens lived, right? Do you think we will get to see pictures on the Internet of these places?" This catches his classmate Luis's attention. "What are you talking about, Jesse? What kings and queens? Did they live in big castles and all that? Boy, would I love to see that. I saw this show one time that . . ." At this point, Mr. Little interjects, "Now wait guys, you know we have to turn to our next activity. However, we will continue our discussion on the continents tomorrow. So, I would appreciate everyone pulling out your list of spelling words."

It is three days later, and the class is involved in a cooperative learning activity. One group of students is talking about the upcoming unit test. "I don't know about all of you, but I am going to study real hard for the test on Friday. I would really like another homework pass. I hate having to do homework all the time. There's so much of it!" Andrea shares. Another student, Lydia, offers a different perspective. "My mom doesn't care much anyway as long as I keep up my test grades and stuff. Besides, I am much better at the presentations Mr. Little has us do. You know, where we get to make charts and pictures and stuff? I am great at putting that stuff together on my computer at home." (Andrea nods her head excitedly in agreement.) "So, I don't care about those passes. Now a pizza party, that would have been really cool." Andrea shakes her head and states, "Well, it's not like you have to study all that much. You don't have to get a perfect score to get the pass, just a 90. What about you, Luis?" Luis pauses before responding, "I don't know. It's cool and everything I guess. But, it only gets you out of one little assignment. Besides, I get a pass every week. It won't be a big deal if I don't get it this time." Sharice nods in agreement. "Don't get me wrong, I can see how everyone likes them and all. But this stuff is kinda cool. I don't know that much about people in other parts of the world. The homework gives me a chance to learn more about all the countries."

It is Monday morning, before class has started, and Mr. Little is reviewing his roll book. He notices that students' grades have been good and decides it may be time to start weaning the kids off the extrinsic rewards this week. Students are starting to file in and he gets up to start the class. "Class, as usual I am proud of all of you who got an A on this week's test. However, next week we're going to do something a little different. Only those students who get a perfect score will receive the no-homework pass. You have all been doing so well, I feel it is time to up the ante, so to speak." (Noticeable groans occur throughout the class.) "That's not fair, Mr. Little. What about those of us who do pretty good? We're not going to get anything?" complains Andrea. Another student, Derek, pipes up, "Yeah, I agree with Andrea. What are we gonna get instead? Some of us just can't get the best scores all the time." (At this point the whole class starts talking about this new state of affairs and Mr. Little is a little concerned about his decision to alter the criteria.) Although he is a bit unsure about the class's reaction, he proceeds, "Well, class, I am not sure about that. Let's just try this new plan for now."

Two weeks have passed, and Mr. Little is growing more concerned about the way many of the students are responding to the change in criteria that earns the no-homework pass. Many are visibly upset when he hands out the no-homework passes. He has also noticed that not as many students are earning the pass, and grades have noticeably dropped on the last two tests. He has even received phone calls from upset parents who feel the new criteria are unfair because their children are at a disadvantage for earning class incentives. So Mr. Little decides to consult some of his colleagues during his planning period in the faculty lounge. "I thought I was doing everything right. You start the rewards off generously and then wean them off, right? Isn't that what those schedules of reinforcement are all about?" Another teacher, Mr. Murphy, shakes his head knowingly. "Well, I hear you. From the start of the school year, I have kids who expect some kind of return on their learning. If I introduce an assignment or project, they ask, 'What's in it for me?'" Another teacher, Mrs. Payne, has been following the conversation and hesitantly offers her opinion, "Personally, I respect that other teachers use such incentives to motivate their students, but I wonder if they aren't overused, so much so that kids rely on them. They don't seem to get the concept of learning for the sake of learning."

Mr. Little has listened attentively to this exchange but now becomes more animated. "Well, do you think I should have been more sparing in my use of rewards? I still think the no-homework pass is a good idea because it worked so well in the beginning. The trouble started when I made the criteria for earning the pass more difficult." Mrs. Payne replies, "Maybe the students see the tougher criteria as unfair. Maybe this allows only the higher-ability students the opportunity to earn the reward." Mr. Little tries to rein in his frustration before replying, "That's exactly what some of my students' parents have complained about! I have even noticed that this whole troublesome issue has led to interruptions during instruction time, and I know I am going to have to set up at least a few parent-teacher conferences! What should I do now?"

DISCUSSION TOPICS

1. Extrinsic Motivation

    a. What are diverse types of reinforcement that teachers can make use of in the classroom? What is a reinforcement menu?

    b. What are schedules of reinforcement? Designate which schedules a teacher should use to reduce the likelihood of extinguishing desirable behavior.

c. Ascertain how extrinsic rewards might be utilized in a more comprehensive classroom management approach in Mr. Little's class.

d. Assess the pros and cons of using external reinforcers in the classroom. Should students be rewarded for learning?

e. Evaluate the argument surrounding whether homework passes should be used in the classroom as a reward.

2. *Intrinsic Motivation*

a. Are there any instances of intrinsic motivation among the students in Mr. Little's class?

b. How could Mr. Little have capitalized on his students' intrinsic motivation during his instruction?

c. Point out how this teacher could have made learning meaningful by building on prior knowledge.

d. Determine what role classroom technology can play in encouraging students' intrinsic motivation to learn.

e. How can humor, personal experiences, and anecdotes show the human side of academic content and foster intrinsic motivation?

f. What original sources can Mr. Little expose his students to in order to communicate important academic content while sparking student interest?

g. Suggest ways that teachers can allow for student choice in their learning, given curriculum constraints.

3. *Goal Orientations*

a. What are mastery and performance goals? Do you see evidence of either type of goal in this case?

    b. How might classroom structure influence such motivational patterns?

    c. How can teachers structure the classroom to create a mastery orientation in their students?

    d. Evaluate whether performance goals are always bad.

4. *Parent Involvement*

    a. How might home–school communication have been of benefit in this case? How can home–school partnerships impact student motivation to learn?

    b. Identify effective ways to facilitate home–school communication.

    c. Develop a list of tips for effective parent–teacher conferencing.

    d. Recommend how a teacher might go about increasing parents' involvement in their children's schooling.

Giving Up

Suggested Theories/Content: Self-Efficacy, Attribution Theory, Learned Helplessness, and Goal Orientations

It is the sixth week of class and Mrs. Reynolds, the newest addition to the algebra department at Lakeview Middle, takes a moment from grading papers to look up at her second-period algebra class, busy working on this week's test. She pauses in her perusal when she notices Anne Sedgewick looking hopelessly out the window. Mrs. Reynolds waits to make eye contact with Anne and at that point the student immediately returns to her test. Mrs. Reynolds inwardly sighs in frustration, because this is not the first instance of Anne's lack of attention to her schoolwork.

The next day, Mrs. Reynolds asks the class to quickly make their way to their seats, for they have much to cover before the end of the period. "OK, class, I am going to pass out the test from yesterday. . ." Mrs. Reynolds begins but is shortly interrupted by William, one of her more boisterous students. "Oh, yeah, let me see my grade, I know all of you punks aren't going to touch my grade this time. I studied my. . ." Before he can finish his sentence, Mrs. Reynolds cuts him off. She glances pointedly at William to stifle further interruptions. "Needless to say, I am really disappointed in some of you. There are two of you—I have it noted on your tests—I need to see after class because your answers look an awful lot alike." Many students begin to giggle and point fingers in the direction of the likely culprits. "However," Mrs. Reynolds continues, "I don't want to waste class time pointing fingers and complaining about the sorry state of your test scores; we need to keep on schedule and turn to the current lesson today. I don't need to reemphasize how important this lesson is for the final at the end of the year as well as the upcoming SATs." At this point, Mrs. Reynolds has made her way to Anne's desk. As she hands Anne her paper, Anne grabs it and quickly flips it over before anyone can see her grade. Mrs. Reynolds notes that Anne furtively glances around to see if anyone might have noticed her grade.

As Mrs. Reynolds attempts to begin the day's discussion on quadratic equations, she has to make repeated requests for students to put away their tests from the day before. She tries to hide her frustration with two students in the back of the classroom who are busy comparing their grades. Once the two students notice the teacher's attention is on them, they quickly give each other one last friendly "shove" and then straighten in their seats. "Now, class, I am going to give you the opportunity to get into your peer groups to work on today's problems. Each group is going to be responsible for one problem from the worksheet." Mrs. Reynolds begins to pass out the worksheet while students move about into their preassigned groups. "I'll give you a moment to look over these problems," she continues, "and then I'll start recording which problems each group volunteers to work on."

Mrs. Reynolds allows the groups to take a few minutes to discuss the worksheets. She circles around to observe Anne's group. The unofficial group leader, Lilly Mitchells, engages the group with her usual take-charge attitude, "I think we should do the fourth problem, it is just like the one we learned about last week and I know we can do it." A couple of the group members agree, but Mrs. Reynolds notices that Anne remains uninvolved other than to drop her eyes and nod her head in mute acknowledgment. One of the group members dares to disagree. "Well, what are we going to learn if we do that, what if one of these other problems is on the next test? I don't know about any of you, but I got a lousy C on yesterday's test." At this point, Mrs. Reynolds notices that most of the groups are starting to socialize and realizes they have had enough time to consider their choice of problem. She directs the class to begin solving their problems as she walks to her desk to finish sorting through some cumulative files.

As the period draws to an end, Mrs. Reynolds asks students to make their way back to their original seats. Within moments, the bell rings and most of the students are off like a shot to make the most of their few precious moments in between classes. She notices Anne hesitating as she packs up her books and makes her way over to the student. "Anne, is there something amiss? Don't you have to get to your third-period class?" Anne appears to wrestle with something, but then breaks down and begins to unload her worries over her academic performance and her grades, in Mrs. Reynolds's class in particular. "I just can't get another bad grade or my parents will lock me up and throw away the key. I just can't imagine getting in anymore trouble than I already am!" Mrs. Reynolds responds, "But Anne, you have never once asked for my help, and I always notice you staring out the window." At this point, Anne seems to become quite calm, looks out the window as if coming to a conclusion she had been avoiding, and then looks up at Mrs. Reynolds. "I try and try, but it just doesn't matter, I am not good at this algebra stuff and there is no getting around that. I should really ask myself why I even bother." "Now hold on a minute, Anne," Mrs. Reynolds interjects, "I know you can do this work. I have faith in you. Plus, look at Loralee, Edith, and Isabelle . . . they are good friends of yours, right? They get strong grades in this class. If they can do it, so can you." Anne smiles but glances down at her watch, realizing what time it is. "Listen, I appreciate your help, but I don't want to add after-school detention for being tardy to Mr. Lopez's Spanish class to my glorified record." As

Anne leaves, Mrs. Reynolds sighs and shakes her head as she realizes the two students asked to stay after class have fled the proverbial scene of the crime.

A month later, Mrs. Reynolds is grading the most recent unit tests. When she gets to Anne Sedgewick's, she skims over the answers and closes her eyes in frustration. Without finishing the grading of the test, she realizes that Anne is going to be less than pleased with the score. She had hoped to see an improvement in Anne's score after their little chat a month prior. But, apparently it hadn't made much of a difference. As she looks back on it, she begins to wonder at her naiveté in thinking such superficial feedback would have seriously helped Anne. Anne clearly had strong perceived inadequacies where this subject matter was concerned, and Anne's sense of hopelessness over the weeks since their chat had only become more evident. Anne hardly ever volunteered to answer questions in class, asked for no further help, and continued to daydream in class. Even on the few occasions she went to Anne's desk to check up on her work, Anne would make halfhearted attempts in her work without really trying to apply herself to the task. Mrs. Reynolds asks herself, what she is supposed to do now. How can she reach this student and help her see that this situation doesn't have to be as hopeless as it appears?

DISCUSSION TOPICS

1. *Self-Efficacy*

    a. What influences students' efficacy?

    b. How do beliefs about ability affect a student's motivation?

    c. What is self-efficacy and how does it differ from one's self-esteem?

d. What are specific metacognitive strategies that teachers can share with students and that would help students study more effectively?

e. Analyze the role of anxiety in learning. Is anxiety always detrimental to learning?

f. Recommend how you would suggest that Mrs. Reynolds go about nurturing Anne's self-efficacy where algebra is concerned.

2. *Attributional Theory*

a. How would you describe Anne's attributional style?

b. How does locus of causality apply to motivation?

c. Classify Anne's attribution along the three dimensions proposed by Weiner.

d. What is learned helplessness? Do you think Anne's behavior fits into the characteristics of those with learned helplessness?

e. Outline proven steps Mrs. Reynolds might try in order to retrain Anne's attributional style.

f. Compile a list of strategies for how teachers can support self-determination and autonomy in students.

3. *Goal Orientations*

a. What are typical student outcomes associated with each type of goal orientation?

b. Separate the different mastery and performance orientations. Do you see evidence of either in this case?

c. How do teachers go about promoting mastery orientation in their classroom? How does Ames' TARGET model for supporting student motivation apply?

d. Distinguish incremental versus entity views on intelligence. Which would you say Anne's espouses?

e.   Relate the concept of the meaningfulness of learning to a mastery orientation among students.

f.   Examine the role of assessment in influencing the type of goal orientation students adopt.

g.   Assess which kinds of goals are the most motivating for students. Are performance goals necessarily always maladaptive to students' learning?

To Belong or Not to Belong

Suggested Theories/Content: Maslow's Need Hierarchy, Adolescent Development

Mike Turner is a tenth-grade teacher with a few years of teaching experience under his belt. He is a well-liked faculty member at the school, and he is known for establishing excellent rapport with students. He teaches English literature, and on more than one occasion, he is seen hauling props to complement his instruction of the latest reading assignment. Many teachers respect his enthusiasm and his talent for engaging otherwise recalcitrant students.

It is the third week of school and Mr. Turner is waiting for his fourth-period literature class to make their way into class and many students are returning from their lunch periods. Mr. Turner has structured his classroom such that his desk is situated at the back of the classroom. As he is gathers his handouts for the upcoming assignment from his desk, he notices Gina Simmons coming into the classroom. Gina is noted for being one of the school's "Goth" set, who dress in dark colors, have noticeably dyed-black hair, and wear only a very dark smattering of black eyeliner. Mr. Turner also knows that Gina will be one of his top students, if her poignant class responses and initial homework assignment grades are any indication. He secretly smiles at her choice of T-shirt today, a black one that claims, "I see stupid people." He wonders if the "hall guard," his name for the administration person who polices the hallways for discipline issues, has noticed Gina's selection of attire for the day. Before he gets further in his musings, he notices that a tightly knit group of girls, and Lila in particular, are observing Gina's entrance too. The clique immediately begins to whisper and engage in obvious snickering at Gina. Mr. Turner takes that opportunity to walk by Lila's desk as he makes his way to the front of the classroom. Predictably, the girls cease their discussion. Mr. Turner moves to the front row and begins passing out the week's upcoming assignment on *Hamlet*.

A few days later Mr. Turner is concluding a class discussion on the interaction between Hamlet and Ophelia that occurs in the third act when Gina begins to offer a comment. "Well, you know, Mr. Turner, I read that act very carefully because . . ." Lila sarcastically interrupts, "I'm surprised you had time to read the assigned pages, especially since you obviously spend so much time hanging out with your Goth friends talking about music, smoking, and discussing where the next party is going to be." The looks of condescension and dislike coming from Lila's friends are an obvious show of support for Lila's offensive. Gina noticeably tenses, but her facial expression barely changes and she replies, "How would you know what we talk about? You are too scared to step out of your small little world to even listen to what other people might be interested in just because they look a little different than you." Mr. Turner watches as the rest of the class turn with interest to any forthcoming invectives from Lila's crew. Before the situation can escalate, he reminds everyone of the merits of camaraderie in their shared learning endeavor in his classroom, and that he adamantly discourages any disrespectful comments. He says this with a pointed look at Lila. He then quickly moves forward in the lesson, making a mental note to look a bit deeper into this issue.

At end of the week, Mr. Turner is grading the students' writing assignment on *Hamlet*. Mr. Turner is looking over the typical distribution of grades and notices that the students who always seem to have trouble are still having trouble. He is reflecting on some way to reach these students, but the truth is he is not sure where the problem lies. Are they truly having trouble grasping the subtleties of English literature, or are they simply not finishing the reading? As he reflects on possible instructional strategies available to him, he also factors in the ongoing tension between Gina and Lila's camp. And as much as Gina seems to do well with the subtleties of Shakespearean literature, she increasingly disengages from classroom discussion just to avoid confrontations that she knows the whole class will be audience to. Clearly, the other students in the class are not willing to stand up to Lila and her friends, and the result is that Gina is rather ostracized within the classroom. Just yesterday, another altercation erupted between Gina and Sharon, one of the other members of Lila's clique. Gina made a derogatory comment about Sharon's "boy-obsession" with the school heartthrob Justin Drake. Obviously their sentiments this time run too deep for Mr. Turner's typical approach—distracting them with the wonders literature has to offer—to work. And, technically, the hostilities are always just inside of the rules of the classroom, so he really doesn't have a classroom management issue so much as an atmosphere of dislike that is beginning to distract the class and is certainly creating a negative learning atmosphere. He decides to take the issue home and mull it over a bit more.

Later that day, Mike Turner is walking down the main hallway to the faculty parking lot when he encounters one of his colleagues, Ned Reilly. After the typical banter associated with the end of a school day, Mike fills Ned in on the situation between the girls and his concerns about Gina's sense of academic comfort in his classroom. As they reach the door to the parking lot, Ned pauses and looks at Mike. Mike observes that Ned doesn't seem surprised. In fact, Ned is quite familiar with Lila and her clique. He tells Mike, "Don't forget, Mike, you've got them right at the beginning of their high school transition. This is a tricky time for them. You see, I have Lila in my second-period geometry course. In my class, Lila sharpens her claws on another female student who is a bit overweight. These students are confronted with puberty and body image issues and an interest in the opposite sex all at the same time. They are also used to being the top dogs in middle school, and now they are on the lowest rung of the ladder, so to speak, with the older high school grades. And, as they try to figure out who they are and where they fit in, they are also trying to distance themselves from their parents. It is no wonder that these tensions arise." Mike sets his briefcase down for a moment to rub his eyes while Ned continues. "And it is no wonder that their motivations lie elsewhere! You are trying to engage them in thoughtful discussions of Hamlet's plight, but there are obviously numerous preoccupations competing with you for their attention."

Mike looks up at Ned and offers, "You know, I have already been considering the idea of cooperative learning to cure another problem I have. A handful of students are just not doing well in my class. So, I have been thinking about establishing some heterogeneous-group learning exercises to allow for some peer scaffolding. Given the research literature on cooperative learning that points to positive social outcomes, attitudes, and social skills, maybe I can cure two ills at the same time after all. Maybe, if I can get them involved in a common cause, they will be able to relate better with each other, especially if I break up Lila's group and place those having trouble with the academic concepts with students who have had stellar performance so far." Mike gazes off as he considers the possibilities.

Before he completely loses Mike to his musings, Ned adds, "I was reading a report that discussed the benefits of cooperative learning activities; it even addressed the importance of involving parents and community leaders in the school. I wonder how that could best be accomplished with high school students?" Mike warms to the new topic, but with skepticism, "Sounds like strategies geared at two different levels—what I can do in my classroom and what we could do on a schoolwide level. Certainly I can't cure the ills of teaching at the high school level all by myself, now, can I?" "Well," Ned considers, "from the rep you seem to have picked up from both faculty and students, I expect you can, so why don't you let me know when you figure it all out." Ned grins mischievously, clearly amused with his witty comment. Mike chuckles at his friend's gibe. "Cute, Ned, whatever happened to collegiality? In any event, I am not sure about parent and community involvement at the high school level. This has always been difficult. I'm good, but not that good." Ned opens the door to his car while looking over his shoulder and remarks, "You mean there's hope for the rest of us after all?" Both men have a laugh over this. "No, seriously," Ned continues, "why don't you bring it up at the next faculty meeting? Seems that the faculty has been toying with the idea of how to get more parents and the community involved for some time now. The assistant principal has been considering an idea for developing a program of parent mentors during after-school hours. You should get her feedback as well. Who knows what we might come up with when we all put our heads together?"

DISCUSSION TOPICS

1. *Maslow's Need Hierarchy*

a. What level of Maslow's Need Hierarchy might be prevalent for the students in this case?

b. Explain how teachers can help students who are motivated by needs to belong or needs for esteem.

c. Given the research on cooperative learning, how might it be used to address deficiencies at either the belonging or esteem level of Maslow's hierarchy?

d. Point out some possibilities for teachers to establish an incentive for students to cooperate in these learning groups.

e. Outline the elements necessary for cooperative learning to be effective.

2. *Adolescent Development*

a. What developmental issues are students facing at these ages?

b. Describe how the increased concern with body image and the relationships with the opposite sex might interfere with academic motivation.

c. Anticipate how teachers might respond to student cliques and the inevitable consequence of some students feeling left out.

d. Debate which stage of Erikson's theory you think applies to the students in this case. How might teachers' awareness of Erikson's theory impact their classroom-teacher decision making?

3. *Parent Involvement*

a. How can teachers increase parent involvement at the high school level?

b. Explain why teachers tend to see drops in parent involvement at the high school level.

c. Decide on ways in which parents might realistically be involved in the high school that would be comfortable for both parents and students. In particular, in what ways might parents serve as coaches or mentors to adolescents?

PART V

Classroom Management

CASE 20: Interruptions

Synopsis: A second grade teacher has trouble keeping her students on task as she deals with a series of misbehaviors.

CASE 21: Parents' Night

Synopsis: A middle school teacher conducts an open house for the parents of her eighth-grade students while successfully accommodating parents who do not speak English. Although she prepares for a night filled with information about content and class procedures and actively engages the parents through several exercises, the question of parent involvement at the middle school level is still raised.

CASE 22: The Rule Breaker

Synopsis: An elementary school teacher's tolerance for misbehavior is tested when a student refuses to follow the class rules despite the teacher's efforts to teach the rules and have students learn by examples. The teacher must resort to behavior management techniques in order to handle the frequent encounters with this student's preference for misbehavior.

VIDEO CLIP 10: Classroom Management

Video Synopsis: In this video, teachers show how active learning engages students, eliminating classroom management problems.

CASE 23: Purposeful Deliberations

Synopsis: Several teachers' instructional approaches are compared when a group of high school students strike up a discussion in the cafeteria about the strengths and weaknesses associated with their classes as well as what aspects of different classes they enjoy most.

Interruptions

Suggested Theories/Content: Behaviorism, Classroom Management, Social Cognitive Theory, and Motivation

Ms. Saks's second-grade class is coming back from lunch and as usual they do not want to settle down and begin their afternoon activities. "Children," Ms. Saks says as she rings the small bell on her desk, "let's get to our desks and begin our spelling lesson. Let's not waste time. Remember, you can earn pegs on the pegboard for good behavior. We all agreed that every student who has five pegs at the end of the week gets a chance at the grab bag." The children seem to want to earn the pegs, for they rapidly find their desks as Ms. Saks rings the bell a second time. By the time she rings the bell a third time, all the students are quietly seated at their desks and are working on spelling problems out of their books. Ms. Saks decides to reward a few of the students for following orders, and puts pegs on the pegboard next to their names. The students are ecstatic. Ms. Saks feels a sense of relief because she believes that she may finally be able to get her students to listen by using this tactic.

Later that day, as Ms. Saks is getting ready to hand out last night's spelling homework, she hears a commotion in the back of the room. Two of her students, Margo and Alice, are heatedly arguing and have now interrupted most of the other students, who are staring at the two girls rather than working on their spelling problems. "What is going on?" Ms. Saks asks as she steps between them. "She started it! She is just a . . ." says Margo and Ms. Saks interrupts, "Now, girls, either we talk calmly about what the problem is, making sure we use our inside voices, or you both get back to your seats." Neither girl answers Ms. Saks but they do head back to their seats.

Ms. Saks is almost finished returning the students' homework when she sees Richard hit Luke. "Richard!" she yells and then asks, "Why did you hit Luke?" "Ms. Saks, you just didn't see him hit me first, I just hit him back, I was just defending myself!" Richard answers. "Nah-ah, Ms. Saks, I didn't hit him at all, he just hit me!" Luke says. "Richard, there is no hitting in the classroom, remember that is rule number four: we keep our hands to ourselves. You will be spending your recess time with me tomorrow," Ms. Saks says. "Oh, but Ms. Saks . . ." Richard whines and throws his hands in the air. Before Ms. Saks can respond to Richard, she notices Margo passing a note to Thalia and motioning for her to pass it on to Alice. Ms. Saks walks over to Thalia's desk and says, "Thalia, what did Margo just give you?" "Um, well," Thalia answers. "Give it to me, please," Ms. Saks says. Thalia hands the note over as Margo calls her a jerk under her breath. "Now get back to work, Thalia," Ms. Saks says and continues in a firm voice, "Margo we do not pass notes in class, and we do not call classmates names, so go over to the good behavior board and remove two of the pegs that are next to your name. You have just lost two of your good behavior pegs for the day." "Oh, but Ms. Saks, I only needed one more to get a chance at the grab bag, and now I'll have to get three more before the week ends!" Margo whines and pouts. "Well," Ms. Saks says, "that is something you should have thought about before misbehaving."

Later that day, Ms. Saks tries to get the class organized into their writing groups. The students will be finishing the short stories they began the day before, and Ms. Saks hopes that there will be enough time for all the groups to complete the assignment because they are running behind schedule today and she prefers not to take time away from the math lesson again. However, Ms. Saks's fear is soon confirmed when, a few minutes into the assignment, two students begin to argue. Although she tries to intercede, in the end she has to remove one of the students' previously earned privileges in order to end to argument.

Ms. Saks then notices as she walks around to check the students' progress that Antonio is off task. "Antonio, that drawing is beautiful but you need to put it away and start contributing to your group's story," Ms. Saks says. "But, Ms. Saks, when Julia was drawing yesterday, you didn't tell her to put it away!" Antonio protests. "Well, that was different, now don't argue with me or you'll be punished," replies Ms. Saks as she is walking away. Ms. Saks is visibly flustered by what Antonio has just said but hopes the students do not notice. Before she has a chance to reach the next group of students she hears Antonio's group arguing. "You are such a baby; besides, it isn't like you are a good speller, you need all the practice in the world," says Julia in a low voice. The other students in the group begin to giggle. Maty adds, "Yeah, you are so dumb Antonio, my baby brother is better at school than you are." "Shut up you morons!" shouts Antonio angrily.

Ms. Saks is forced to handle the escalating problem. She decides to take away more privileges. "Maty, you have just lost a good behavior sticker. Julia and Antonio, you no longer have a chance to participate in the class raffle and you will all now work independently, so move your desks back to their original position and get back to work." "But it is not fair! You are always on their side, I hate you, I hate all of you!" shouts Antonio furiously as he pushes his chair forcibly and the chair falls over and lands with a loud crashing sound. Ms. Saks tries to remain calm for she knows that all the students are watching this incident carefully. "Antonio, you need to stop arguing and get to work; otherwise I am afraid that you are going to lose one of your chances for a homework pass." Antonio is not listening; instead he begins to yell obscenities and heads toward the door.

DISCUSSION TOPICS

1. *Behaviorism*

a. From the perspective of operant conditioning, what types of continuous reinforcement and/or intermittent reinforcement is Ms. Saks using?

b. Distinguish between continuous and intermittent reinforcement. Outline their advantages and disadvantages and their effect on behavior.

c. Identify and discuss the types of punishments Ms. Saks is using.

d. Judge whether Ms. Saks is using reinforcement/punishment effectively. If not, suggest how such reinforcers/punishers can be used effectively to manage student behaviors.

e. Summarize what other Skinnerian behavior modification techniques are available to teachers in managing their classrooms.

f. From the perspective of Behaviorism, what are the advantages and disadvantages of using applied behavioral analyses as a means for managing behavior in the classroom?

2. *Classroom Management*

a. Explain how Ms. Saks's management strategies might be organized into a more comprehensive classroom management model like Canter's Assertive Discipline. What constitutes a Classroom Discipline Plan?

b. Illustrate how disturbances in the classroom relate to Kounin's constructs of withitness, teacher desists, overlappingness, maintaining focus, and smoothness and momentum.

c. Differentiate between the various ways to handle aggression in the classroom. Suggest which approaches might be more suitable for handling Antonio.

3. *Social Cognitive Theory*

    a. Discuss the role that Bandura's social cognitive theory plays in this case. In particular, justify how vicarious reinforcement and punishment may be evident in this case.

    b. Relate whether Ms. Saks is using observational learning in her classroom. Outline suggestions for using observational learning in this classroom.

4. *Motivation*

    a. Identify the different motivational constructs that may be used in this classroom. Which ones are Ms. Saks using? Are they being employed effectively?

    b. Explain how certain motivational strategies may be more effective with this age group. Suggest techniques that detail such motivational constructs.

    c. In relation to student motivation, what are the potential problems of using extrinsic reinforcers in the classroom?

Parents' Night

Suggested Theories/Content: Home–School Communication, Classroom Management, and Bilingualism

Kimberly Wheaton is getting ready for Parents' Night with her eighth graders. She is anxious to meet her students' families because she strongly believes that the parent–teacher partnership aids student achievement and behavior. She glances around her room, ensuring that all the activities she plans on doing are in the right sequence on her desk and that all the packets of handouts have the correct sheets in them. Mercedes Davila, her Spanish interpreter, peeks her head in the door. "Hi, Mercedes, please come in." "Hello, Kim, how are the preparations coming along?" Mercedes asks. "Oh great, I was just checking on some last-minute things to avoid getting nervous," Kim explains. "You will do just fine. It is funny how these nights can still be nerve-wracking after years of conducting them," Mercedes answers, and Kim nods in agreement. "Well, I have six Hispanic students, but only four of the six will need your interpreting. The other families, I have been assured, are bilingual. Here are their names and the students' names—oh, and please remind them that I will always try to communicate with them through messages in their native language whenever I am able to do so," Kimberly states, handing Mercedes the list. "I definitely will. Well, I will make myself at home in the back of the classroom," Mercedes says as she walks toward the tables set up in the back of the room.

The parents arrive slowly; they enter the room and begin to look around. Most of them seem unsure of exactly where they should go. "Welcome, please don't be shy, come in take a look around, and when you are ready, please take a seat," Kimberly states excitedly. Some parents immediately greet Kimberly, introduce themselves, and briefly identify who they are here for; other parents are standing and talking to one another while still others have taken their seats. Some of the parents seem to know one another and are greeting each other warmly.

Kimberly begins the open house by introducing herself and discusses what parents can expect their eighth graders to learn in her physical science class. Once she is finished with her introduction of the class to the parents she announces, "Well, now I would like the opportunity to get to know you, so if you would not mind, please introduce yourselves and tell us a little something about you and your family. May I have a volunteer to start us off?" Kimberly asks cheerfully. A parent in the front rises and begins to speak about herself and her son. Soon after, another parent follows and before long, all the parents including the Hispanic parents—with Mercedes' help—have introduced themselves.

Kimberly distributes sample assignments for parent, to see and explains the requirements of each assignment. She makes sure to glance at Mercedes often to verify that the parents seated with her are following along and that she may continue at this pace. Mercedes indicates with a thumb up if she is going at a good pace or down if Kimberly is to slow down to give Mercedes a chance to catch them up. Kimberly also makes sure to discuss behavior and explain her classroom management strategies. She directs parents to the page containing the class rules in the packet she has prepared for them. They also converse about the samples in the packet of positive and negative notes that she would send home to signal their children's progress. In addition, she asks parents to give an example of how a student in this class could "break" one of the class rules and then explain the consequence that student would face. Most of the parents really seem to be enjoying themselves and seem appreciative that they can experience directly what may happen to their sons or daughters in this class. A parent expresses his disbelief that this type of open house is offered for eighth graders. He is used to parent involvement being reduced to a minimum once a child enters middle school. Kimberly agrees that this is a typical view but that her wishes are for parents to increase their involvement in the secondary years because it is fundamental to student learning and achievement. She is a strong advocate of parents being involved in school throughout their children's education. She then discusses several different ways that parents can become involved in her classroom, informs them that she will send notices home of activities that will be taking place and in which she would like parent volunteers, and says she hopes they will all respond.

Kimberly then directs the parents' attention to the bulletin board to the left of the class, on which she has listed a series of techniques for rewarding students for their accomplishments. She discusses each technique with them and then asks for volunteers to offer examples of how they celebrate accomplishments in their homes. She is happy to see that Mercedes has raised her hand indicating that she is going to be translating for one of the parents seated with her. "Yes, please go ahead," Kimberly says as most of the parents turn in their seats to direct their attention to the back of the classroom. "In her home [she motions to the parent sitting immediately to her left], she normally cooks the child's favorite meal and then lets the child choose what the whole family will have for dessert," Mercedes says. Many of the parents nod in agreement and some say this is a good idea. Another parent raises her hand and tells the class that she allows her daughter to skip her chores, and another informs the class that her son receives an increase in spending money for that week. Kimberly is pleased that so many parents are volunteering suggestions, especially since the suggestions are appropriate for all socio-economic levels.

Kimberly feels that this open house has been an outrageous success. She had a 70 percent turnout and all the parents were receptive, provided her with contact numbers and email addresses and said to contact them if she ever needed to. Kimberly ends with a gift bag she has prepared for each family. The bag contains a magnet that she created out of the list of assignments, due dates, and exam dates as well as "tip sheets" for the parents and for the students. These "tip sheets" consist of helpful hints for the student on how to complete each assignment successfully and ideas for the parents on how they can help their children with the assignments. Many parents personally thank her and say they look forward to meeting her on another occasion.

DISCUSSION TOPICS

1. *Home–School Communication*

   a. Conclude how conducting this open-house night may improve home–school communication for Kimberly Wheaton.

   b. Discuss the methods that Kimberly Wheaton uses to ensure that the parents feel comfortable and at ease.

   c. Justify the importance of making parents aware of good citizenship examples and how they are being employed in the classroom and at home. Judge the effectiveness of having parents cite examples of rewards in their home.

   d. Explain how home–school partnerships impact student motivation to learn.

   e. Devise effective ways to facilitate home–school communication. Relate how Kimberly Wheaton may have used these ways in her classroom.

f. Compile ways a teacher can increase parents' involvement in their children's schooling.

g. Support the conclusion that research on parent involvement has found that home–school communication usually decreases with older students. Generate examples of ways teachers might continue such communication and involvement.

2. *Classroom Management*

a. Describe how Kimberly Wheaton's efforts to share classroom management strategies, assignments, and so on, aid in any parent–teacher conferences she may have to schedule.

b. Outline tips you could extend to Kimberly Wheaton for effective parent–teacher conferencing.

c. Conclude whether Kimberly Wheaton has communicated her expectations and the rules of the class effectively. Rate her approaches and discuss others that may be effective.

d. From the case, infer what Kimberly Wheaton's approach to classroom management is likely to be.

3. *Bilingualism*

a. Explain the term *bilingualism*. Discuss the theoretical underpinnings of this body of research.

b. Justify how having an interpreter may aid Kimberly Wheaton's open house.

c. Illustrate the importance of attempting to communicate in the parent's native language.

d. Compose a list that shows the range of options available to teachers in communicating with parents who don't speak English.

e. Generate arguments that discuss whether teacher preparation programs typically prepare teachers for this aspect of teaching. How might preparation be made even more effective?

CASE 22

The Rule Breaker

 VIDEO: Classroom Management
located at *mylabschool.com*

Suggested Theories/Content: Classroom Management, Behaviorism, Social Cognitive Theory, and Cognitive Development

Ms. Atista's second-grade class is sitting on the carpet at the back of the room in a semicircle while Ms. Atista sits on a stool next to a large bulletin board. For the first ten minutes of every day, the class discusses the class rules. It is the beginning of the school year and Ms. Atista wants to ensure that all the students know the rules as well as the consequences for breaking rules. On the first day of school and in addition to the rules she has created for the class, Ms. Atista allows the students to produce some of their own and, as a class, they decide which ones they should add. Today the class is reviewing the rules and coming up with examples of how each rule can be broken.

They have gone through rules one and two when a student raises his hand. "Do you have a question, Edwin?" Ms. Atista asks. The student whose hand was raised nods his head. "Good job on raising your hand. You have just demonstrated how not to break rule number two, which is not to speak while another is speaking but to raise your hand until I call on you. Very good, Edwin! Now, go ahead with your question, please," Ms. Atista says. "So, if I ran when I got up to get in line, I would be in trouble because of rule number three?" asks Edwin. "You would not be in trouble, Edwin, but you would have broken rule number three. Can anyone tell me what this rule is?" asks Ms. Atista, pointing to rule number three on the large board titled CLASS RULES in bold red letters. "It is not to run in the classroom!" Harrison shouts excitedly. "Well, I must be imagining things because I thought I heard an answer but I have not called on anyone yet!" Ms. Atista says. Harrison immediately raises his hand and Ms. Atista motions for him to answer the question.

"Now, class, can we think of why rule number four is important?" Ms. Atista asks. Erin raises her hand and Ms. Atista motions for her to speak. "Because we should not be touching other people, because they may not like people to touch them and so we don't touch them." "Very good, Erin. I can see you were paying attention when we discussed our rules, because it is very important to respect others and their space. So, we do not touch others without their permission. Just like we do not take things from others without their permission, which is our next rule, rule number five," Ms. Atista answers. Before the discussion can continue, Ms. Atista walks over to the side of the classroom where there is an area marked "TIME-OUT," and where Ben has been sitting, and motions for Ben to join the rest of the class. Ben immediately tells Ms. Atista that he knew all the answers to the questions she asked the class and then he accuses her of purposely not calling on him even though his hand was raised. Ms. Atista explains to Ben that while in time-out students are not allowed to participate in what the class is doing nor are they allowed to receive any treats or rewards. She then asks Ben, "Did you learn anything from being in time-out?" Ben shakes his head and loudly says, "No!" "Well, that is a shame, Ben," answers Ms. Atista and she continues, "because you are not using your indoor voice and, because you tell me you did not learn how to control yourself better in time-out, you may very well be there again and miss out on all the things that the rest of the class has been doing and learning. Now, go sit down on the carpet and join your classmates." The class continues to go over the rules before beginning their spelling lesson.

Later that day, the class is cleaning up so that they may line up to go to recess. Ms. Atista reminds the class that the students who will get to go first to recess will be the ones who have put all their materials away and are sitting in their seats. While the students are putting their materials away, Ms. Atista notices that Erin and Clarice are pushing each other to try to fit their supplies on the same shelf. Ms. Atista says, "Now remember, class, there is a place for all of the supplies, so there is no need to try to push some other student out of your way in order to get your supplies on a shelf—Erin, Clarice." Both girls glance over at their teacher and find other places for their supplies before returning to their seats.

Soon, Ms. Atista calls the green table and all of the students happily get up and begin to form the line by the door to the playground. "All right, now the blue table may get up and go get in line. Please remember to walk, children, not run, or you will be sitting back down," Ms. Atista warns. All the students belonging to the blue table follow the teacher's instructions except for Ben, who runs to get in line and knocks Stacey down. "Ben, please come here. The rest of the tables, please line up, and then, line leader, please take the line out to recess." The line leader, Javier, smiles at Ms. Atista and begins to walk out of the class with the rest of his classmates following behind. "Now, Ben, you deliberately disobeyed me when I said to walk to get in line. This is the fourth time today that you have broken one of the class rules. I am sending a note home to your parents about your behavior. If you misbehave again today, you will not be going to recess at all tomorrow. Now, go and sit in time-out until I call you," Ms. Atista says sternly.

Later that day, the class is working on their reading lessons. The class is divided into three reading groups that differ in ability. While Ms. Atista is working with one group, her aide, Kona, is working with another group and the third group is working independently. Ms. Atista's group is taking turns reading aloud. While Harrison is reading, Ms. Atista notices that a problem is beginning in the group that is working with Kona. In order to prevent the situation from escalating, Ms. Atista asks Harrison to continue reading and instructs the rest of the group to follow in the order they have been reading until she returns. "What is going on?" Ms. Atista asks Kona. "Well, Ms. Atista, Ben just marked all over Edwin's paper and when I explained to him that he should apologize, Ben took the paper and ripped it in half," explains Kona holding up Edwin's torn paper. Edwin is visibly upset and explains to Ms. Atista that Ben tore his summary of the story they have been reading. "Ben, what do you have to say?" Ms. Atista asks. "I was just trying to see it, and he did not let me, it isn't my fault, he just wanted to get me in trouble," Ben replies angrily. "Why did you need to see his summary?" Ms. Atista asks, giving Ben a chance to explain, while she looks at the reading group that she was working with and nods for them to go on reading and quickly glances at the group that is independently working. "'Cause," replies Ben. "Because of . . . ?" Ms. Atista asks. "You did not need to be looking at anyone else's summary; you needed to be creating your own, which I see you have not done, Ben," Ms. Atista says, holding Ben's paper, then continues, "I told you earlier that you would be losing recess tomorrow if you misbehaved again, so tomorrow you will not be going out for recess. Now, please get back to work." Ms. Atista returns to the reading group that she had been working with.

At the end of the day, Kona and Ms. Atista talk while they put supplies away. "Wow, Ms. Atista, you are really good, I mean you always know what is happening in the room and sometimes it doesn't even look like you could have seen it. Like when Ben messed up Edwin's story," Kona exclaims.

"Thanks for the compliment. I guess I do stay on top of what is going on. I just believe you can make a difference in all of your students' lives—it is just that with some it is more difficult than with others." Both ladies look at each other and say, "Ben!" in unison. "Well, he is difficult, but so far I have noticed he has his good days and he has his bad days, I am hoping that a letter home to his folks may help with his behavior. Otherwise, I will have to call his parents in for a conference." Ms. Atista says.

DISCUSSION TOPICS

1. *Classroom Management*

   a. Determine which type of Baumrind's classroom management strategies Ms. Atista demonstrates. Rate its effectiveness.

   b. Relate whether Ms. Atista demonstrates "withitness" in the classroom. Support your answers from the case and, if she is not demonstrating "withitness," devise ways that she could.

   c. Determine and justify whether you would classify Ms. Atista's management strategy as a minor or a moderate intervention. Support your answer with examples from the case.

   d. With regard to the physical makeup of the classroom, conclude which type of arrangement style Ms. Atista uses in her classroom. Evaluate its effectiveness with regard to classroom management.

   e. Outline how Ms. Atista uses different techniques in the class to deal with discipline problems. Determine their effectiveness.

   f. Discuss the importance of creating a "community" in the classroom. How does Ms. Atista accomplish that?

g. Explain the importance of having clear, concise rules and ensuring that students understand such rules. Refer to the case.

h. Summarize which classroom management models seem most appropriate for use with second-grade students.

2. *Behaviorism*

a. From the perspective of operant conditioning, differentiate among the types of reinforcement Ms. Atista is using.

b. Illustrate which types of punishments Ms. Atista is using.

c. Judge whether Ms. Atista is using reinforcement/punishment effectively. Discuss the importance of using reinforcers/punishers effectively to manage student behaviors.

d. Generate other Skinnerian behavior modification techniques that are available to teachers in managing their classrooms.

e. From the perspective of Behaviorism, compare and contrast the advantages and disadvantages of using applied behavioral analyses as a means for managing behavior in the classroom.

3. *Social Cognitive Theory*

a. Justify how vicarious reinforcement and punishment may be playing a role in this case.

b. Determine whether Ms. Atista is using observational learning in this case. Should you conclude that she is not, design methods for how Ms. Atista could use observational learning in her class. Generate other techniques that could apply to other classroom situations.

4. *Cognitive Development*

   a. Diagram Piaget's stage of cognitive development that most of Ms. Atista's students are likely to be functioning in.

   b. Relate examples of the students' cognitive development that are evident in this case.

   c. Summarize how students' level of cognitive development would play a role in the types of rules and classroom management techniques that the teacher would successfully employ.

Purposeful Deliberations

Suggested Theories/Content: Teacher-Centered Instruction, Student-Centered Instruction, and Effective Teaching

As Carolina sits in Mrs. Romero's fifth-period geometry class, she cannot wait to begin the day's activities. She knows that Mrs. Romero will be distracted by questions and helping students with specific problems, so she can finish her outline for social studies on the Great Depression, which is due next period. Carolina has figured out that if she can work on her social studies paper during Mrs. Romero's class, she will have it finished by next week and not have to worry about it during the weekends, when all she wants to do is spend time with her friends.

Just as Carolina hoped, Mrs. Romero has asked the students to go about the room and choose a center to begin working at. Mrs. Romero's class is always structured so that students have to choose a station to work at during the beginning of the class, and complete up to three stations in one period if time allows. Each station is centered on a specific topic. The current ones are: Angles and Parallel Lines, Triangles, Polygons and Polyhedra, Circles and Spheres, Surface Area and Volume, Transformations and Symmetry, and Geometric Inequalities and Optimization. Each station has activities set up that encourage discovery, inquiry, and dialogue as well as prepared assignments to test the students' knowledge, and certain criteria that students must meet in order to pass the unit.

Gracie, one of Carolina's best friends, approaches her at the end of the period, after having turned in her work for the day. "What are you doing, girl, that doesn't look like geometry?" asks Gracie. "Oh, you startled me, I am finishing my social studies outline for next period because it is due and I don't want to be out 35 points," answers Carolina as she writes. "Really? Well, what were you doing last night instead of your outline? Isn't that why we got off the phone?" asks Gracie. "I had every intention of doing it but then AJ called and you know how that goes, besides I knew there was always Mrs. Romero's class that I could do it in. Actually, it was AJ who reminded me that he used to do all of his homework in her class and still earned a B." "Aren't you worried that Mrs. Romero will notice that you did not turn in any work?" inquires Gracie frowning. "Nah, Mrs. Romero is so easygoing that I can just tell her I forgot to turn in my work and she'll accept it tomorrow—when I have had a chance to read Reece's notes in seventh period. I mean, he is such a brain!" answers Carolina casually as both girls pack up their belongings and await the bell that signals they may go to lunch. "I have to say, that is pretty sneaky of you because from afar it always looks like you are doing the work. I just can't believe that the information on the centers doesn't interest you any. I mean, some of the way that this work is set up is pretty cool. And it is nice that Mrs. Romero is not always drilling us for information or having us sit there doing seat work like Mr. Bernard does in social studies. I mean, she hardly even gives us any homework, and even when she does it is always applying things, which I happen to think is kinda fun . . . for school work," Gracie says. The bell rings and they both head toward their lockers before going to lunch. "What's up, beautiful women?" Deshon asks as he slips his arms around both girls, who are closing their lockers. "Hi, Deshon. Gracie and I were just heading off to lunch." "Great, wait for me to put these books in my locker and I will walk with you," Deshon says happily as both girls nod and pause to wait for their friend.

In the cafeteria, Carolina, Gracie, and Deshon join other friends, who have already begun eating. "So, Carolina, were you able to do the outline for social studies?" asks AJ, taking a bite of his sandwich. "Oh, yeah, it was no problem," replies Carolina. "You must be talking about Mrs. Romero's class," announces Deshon, taking a sip of his drink as he continues, "I swear, me and AJ, well, actually a lot of us must have done all our other work in there last year and we all passed. I don't think she ever had a clue. It is a shame more classes aren't like hers." Deanna, one of the other students seated at the table, says, "I like Mrs. Romero though; she is such a sweetheart and so knowledgeable. I think the way she sets up her class makes the time go by so fast you don't even feel like you are there to learn. Well, I guess for those of us that are actually doing the assignments and learning, that is." She pauses to wink at AJ and Deshon and continues, "I mean, if I have to sit through another period in Ms. Ellis's English class, I will just scream! We never get to express our opinions; she just lectures, lectures, lectures, and expects us to just listen for the whole hour. Ugh. It is so frustrating." "Oh, tell me about it . . . and what about Mr. Bernard's class?" Gracie asks, not pausing long enough to warrant a reply as she continues, "he has that question-and-answer session, you all know the one—where he gives you about two seconds to answer a question and then he is off to another student." "Yeah, and then he takes away points from your grade for not knowing the answer," Deshon interjects while eating, "I remember that guy. He is a nutcase!" Deshon finishes. The group of students all nod their heads in agreement. Carolina adds, "And I hate how you never know what information Mr. Bernard will ask on the test because his lessons are all over the place. It is like he never knows what he is teaching so it makes it so-o-o-o confusing.

Not to mention he always acts like he does not want to be here, like he is always bored with us or something." Everyone nods in agreement. "Well, I heard that he is getting out of teaching because he is burned out . . . that is what Coach Wilkins told us, right Reece?" asks AJ looking for confirmation from his friend who is sitting directly across from him. "Yeah, that's right! I guess most of our teachers just stink," Reece answers as he peels a banana, and continues, "lucky for me that I'm so smart," Reece finishes with a grin.

"Oh c'mon man, they are not all that bad, Mr. Van Helstic is all right" says Logan, who until now had been too busy chatting with a group of cheerleaders to add to his friends' comments. Logan continues as he sits down to join his friends, "I mean, Mr. Van Helstic talks too, you know, but he has good review sessions that you can pay attention to if you missed something the day before—what does he call them?" Logan asks as he pauses. "Mind refreshers—because they are supposed to refresh your mind from the day before," Carolina answers and continues, "I am sure they come in handy, Logan, especially when you miss something in class because you are too busy drooling over Miranda!" The students all laugh, including Logan, who adds, "Well, it's because she is something to look at, especially since in Mr. Van Helstic's class we have a chance to work in groups. I mean how fresh would that be if she and I get to be in the same group?" Logan asks knowingly as he smiles at his male counterparts, who agree with him, while the female students laugh and roll their eyes. Gracie adds, jokingly tapping Logan on the forearm, "And lucky for you that Mr. Van Helstic also reviews at the end, so people like you can make sure they got all of the right answers." "Today, though, we did something like Mrs. Romero's class—you know, with centers, but unlike Mrs. Romero's class, things are better coordinated and you definitely have to do the work or you get an F for the day," AJ says as the bell rings indicating lunch has ended. The students casually make their way to their next class of the day.

DISCUSSION TOPICS

1. *Teacher-Centered Instruction*

a. Discuss the planning methods when preparing teacher-centered instruction.

b. Explain the approaches that are characteristically associated with teacher-centered instruction.

c. Identify the characteristics of teacher-centered instruction. Which teachers in the case study are using teacher-centered approaches to instruction as described by their students?

d. Summarize how wait time with regard to questioning affects student learning. Describe how questioning can be used effectively. Integrate examples from the case.

e. Outline the potential benefits of using teacher-centered instruction. Diagram what techniques increase the effectiveness of teacher-centered instruction. Explain how these techniques were demonstrated in the case.

f. Discuss the criticisms of teacher-centered instruction—in particular, direct instruction. How is this demonstrated in this case?

g. Explain the role of taxonomies of educational objectives in planning.

2. *Student-Centered Instruction*

a. Compare and contrast the planning methods for student-centered instruction and teacher-centered instruction. Discuss the role of objectives in learner-centered instruction.

b. Outline the teaching methods that are consistent with student-centered instruction.

c. Discuss how learning takes place in student-centered instruction. Which teachers in the case study are using student-centered approaches to instruction as described by their students?

d. Devise the potential benefits of using student-centered instruction. Cite examples from the case.

e. Discuss how Mrs. Romero may have made errors in the way she conducted her lessons. How may her teaching approach be made more effective in reaching all students?

f. Diagram potential problems for designing student-centered instruction.

3. *Effective Teaching*

a. Discuss the general characteristics of effective or good teaching.

b. Describe the teachers in the cases whom the students find effective and discuss what particular methods they may be employing that accounts for their success.

PART VI

Assessment and Evaluation

CASE 24: Standardized Testing: A Call to Arms

Synopsis: Brasswood Elementary School has just completed the practice run-through of the upcoming state achievement tests and the scores are disappointing. During a faculty meeting teachers and administration discuss the school's dismal results on the test, the controversies surrounding such testing, and how to improve their students' performance.

 VIDEO CLIP 11: Standardized Tests

Video Synopsis: Norm-referenced measurement is compared to criterion-referenced measurement of standardized tests. The high-stakes nature of standardized tests may lead many teachers to "teach to the test." Students should be taught how to take a standardized test, but not taught the actual material directly.

CASE 25: Meaningful Classroom Assessment

Synopsis: An experienced teacher tries switching to the alternative portfolio assessment in her twelfth-grade U.S. History class, and she encounters the growing pains of establishing fair grading practices, parental concerns, and inequity in student access to technology.

Standardized Testing:
A Call to Arms

 VIDEO: Standardized Tests
located at *mylabschool.com*

Suggested Theories/Content: Standardized Testing, Teacher's Role in Standardized Testing, Controversies in Testing, Student Preparation

Brasswood Elementary School has just completed the practice run-through of the upcoming state achievement tests and teachers have received a printout of the school's performance by grade level in their faculty mailboxes before the start of the day. It is the end of the day, and teachers are making their way to the faculty meeting that has been called for the express purpose of discussing the school's dismal results on the test.

As the last of the teachers find an empty seat, the assistant principal, Ms. Lui, begins to address the faculty. "Well, ladies and gents, I am sure you all know why we need to meet today. I have already spoken to many of you and I am aware that most of us are clearly stunned by the rather disheartening results from the practice tests. I know we are all in this together and need to figure out how to remedy this situation as best we can before the real tests in just a few months. I hope I don't need to remind anyone just how important these test scores are for the school's image with both parents and the community. And don't get me started on the implications for district attention if we receive failing scores after our rather dismal performance last year! Unfortunately, I don't have the answers here. I want to immediately turn the floor over to open discussion. What are the big factors influencing such poor scores? And more important, what can we do differently? How can we better prepare our students?"

Penelope Johnson, a third-grade teacher, immediately jumps on Ms. Lui's first question, "Ms. Lui, now I know you and I have spoken of this before, but I feel I should bring it up for the benefit of the entire faculty. A real problem that is factoring into many of my students' grades has little to do with achievement and a great deal to do with the fact that their first language is not English. For instance, I have one student who excels in science and mathematics, but he is having difficulty understanding the questions on the test. This raises a real issue as to the validity of these test results. His scores are less a reflection of achievement than a reflection of his hang-up with the English language. And with the great population of immigrant and migrant families in the area, I am sure I am not the only teacher here faced with this contradiction."

Ms. Lui nods her head in acknowledgment of Penelope's statements, "Penelope raises a very important issue with our ESOL (English for Speakers of Other Languages) students. Last year we also had a serious issue with our African American and Latino students scoring lower than the median score. After using the state's revised version of the test, I am happy to say that we have seen a real narrowing in the gap between our different student populations. However, the gap is still there and, unfortunately, the pleas of many administrators across the district have gone unheard in reference to the consideration of performance and portfolio-type assessments to complement these more traditional types of assessments."

Another teacher, Bruce Williams, immediately picks up where Ms. Lui leaves off. "I agree. This happens every year, and it is quite upsetting for parents. Every year I have at least one set of parents who either don't have a solid grasp of English or represent a different ethnic group, visibly upset by these tests. They want to set up conferences to discuss these tests and what the options are for their children. However, I don't want to make it seem like I don't have parents of my middle-class white students who don't get upset about these scores or want to get some questions answered. Recent legislation has focused national attention on these tests and across groups, parents want to understand what their kids are up against."

"Now if you don't mind my asking, Bruce, what do you tell these parents when they ask what they can do at home to help their children?" Penelope questions. I have given some worksheets to parents who are interested, but other than those meager resources the only advice I know to pass along is that staple we all give about being prepared for the test. Things like 'make sure the students have plenty of sleep the night before and a nutritional breakfast.' You know, 'go through the items they are really sure about before working on those they find more challenging.' But it seems there have to be some other options we can give those parents who actively seek to help out at home."

Bruce answers, "Actually, I usually work with parents to help develop their children's metacognitive study skills—skills that are going to be helpful for their academic career in general. But I also feel it helps if parents have a good understanding of what these tests are like. Only then can they really be a resource to their kids. And it is unfortunate, but when you are dealing with parents, many don't even understand what these achievement tests scores mean—the norm-referenced nature of the scores and how the scores are used. And sometimes I am at real loss as to what to tell them. Heck, I don't even agree with the amount of weight that is put on these test scores! And because they carry so much weight, many of us find ourselves sacrificing instructional activities that engage students in higher-level processing or problem-based learning in order to go through yet another set of instructional drills geared toward the state tests."

"Now, I know I am going to be asking for it by mentioning this, but I feel it needs to be said," Marc Diaz tentatively interjects, "let's not throw the baby out with the bathwater here. I agree there are some questionable forces at work as to how these tests scores are used, and maybe too much weight is put on them. However, they are not going away and I don't really think we are truly answering Ms. Lui's question. How can we better prepare our students? What role can these parents play in helping to prepare their children for these tests?"

DISCUSSION TOPICS

1. *Standardized Testing*
    a. Be familiar with key terms associated with standardized testing.
    b. Explain what norms, validity, reliability, and fairness have to do with judging the quality of a standardized test.
    c. Distinguish between construct, content, and criterion validity.
    d. Compare and contrast aptitude versus achievement tests. What does each intend to measure? How are results from these tests typically used?
    e. Distinguish between a norm-referenced and criterion-referenced test. What is one obvious advantage of each type of score over the other?

2. *Role of Teachers and Parents*
    a. Define the technical terms all teachers should be prepared to explain to parents in regard to standardized testing.

b. Prepare some general tips for effective communication during parent conferences that you might offer to teachers like Penelope and Bruce.

c. Analyze the role parents might play in helping their children prepare for standardized tests. How can we involve parents in this manner?

3. *Controversies in Standardized Testing*

a. What are the key controversies that surround standardized testing?

b. What are accommodations in testing that should be made for students whose native language is not English?

c. Analyze what the costs to society might be of using biased standardized tests in the schools. Can you ever free a test completely of cultural influence? If so, how? If not, why not?

d. Should performance assessments accompany standardized tests? What are authentic assessments and what do you think their role should be in achievement testing?

e. Evaluate the main criticisms of state-mandated testing. What are the central issues surrounding the accountability and "high-stakes testing" debate? What are the possible advantages and uses of high-stakes testing?

4. *Student Preparation*

a. How can we better prepare students for standardized testing?

b. What are some metacognitive study skills that we can teach our students?

c. What are important test-taking tips we should communicate to students? How can we help students to become expert test takers?

d. Compose your own advice about standardized testing that you would give to new teachers.

e. Evaluate what the research has to say about "coaching" or training programs designed to help students to do well on a test.

Meaningful Classroom Assessment

Suggested Theories/Content: Traditional versus Alternative Assessment, Portfolio Assessment, and Fair Testing Practices

"OK, now we are talking," Angela Whitaker exhaled. Mrs. Whitaker is a tenured teacher at Horace Mann High School with a wealth of teaching experience under her belt, and during this long teaching campaign, she has become bored and disillusioned with the preponderance of traditional types of classroom assessment. In the last week before the start of the new school year, Mrs. Whitaker put the final touches on her new major classroom assessment method in the form of a portfolio project that would catalogue her twelfth graders' mastery of U.S. history. She gave one more cursory glance to her handout of criteria on the project that outlined each of the major sections of the portfolio: revolution and the Constitution, expansion and reform, Civil War and Reconstruction, industrialization and urbanization, and two final sections on student self-reflection and resources for continued learning.

It is the first day of class and Mrs. Whitaker has just introduced the portfolio project. "So, class, this will represent 75 percent of your grade in the class. You will still have some tests, but the majority of your grade will come from the grades you receive on the portfolio due at intermittent times during the term as outlined on your handout. Now, I want to give you some idea of the materials that might be included in your portfolio. Really expand your thinking on how to demonstrate your mastery! For instance, you might include written essays, concept maps, charts and tables, significant newspaper and magazine clippings, and video/audio recordings of any performance exercises you put together." Miranda, one of her more perfectionist students, raises her hand to say, "But, Mrs. Whitaker, what's this about the last two portfolio sections on self-reflection and resources?" "Good question," Mrs. Whitaker responds while addressing the class at large, "in the self-reflection section I want you to chart your learning progress. Perhaps you could include some journal or self-analysis entries that list stumbling blocks and how you overcame them. Then, in the final section on resources for continued learning, you might keep a running catalogue of books, journals, magazines, email contacts, websites, or other helpful resources as you continue your journey in learning our country's history. I really think everyone will take a great deal more from their learning after this project. Instead of just memorizing some isolated facts, albeit documenting some great points in our history, now you will have the opportunity to engage in critical thinking and problem solving about these issues! Think how much more meaningful this will be than some boring old pencil-and-paper tests. This way, you will be using state-of-the-art word processing and graphics available in the classroom or through your own personal use at home!"

At this point, Miranda raises her hand again. As Mrs. Whitaker inwardly rolls her eyes, she calls on Miranda. "But, Mrs. Whitaker, how will we be graded on this?" Mrs. Whitaker hesitates for a moment and notices that Miranda has now managed to capture the entire class's attention, a feat most teachers would envy. Mrs. Whitaker responds, "Why Miranda, just like any other paper or project would be graded. What I will probably do is to pick out those portfolios that truly represent the best products and use them as samples in which to grade the remaining class projects. Certainly I will be looking for each section to have documentation using a diverse sampling of materials. But that is another good question, Miranda. Maybe what I should do is work on a supplementary handout that will list some criteria before the first upcoming deadline." A few students look skeptical, but most nod their heads and look to the teacher for the next step on the day's agenda.

It is the end of the second week of school, and by the end of the following week the students will be submitting their portfolios for the first time. Mrs. Whitaker is on her way home for the day when she stops in for her messages in the main office of the school. She is surprised to see two slips from concerned parents, including Miranda Jones's mother. She steps into the faculty lounge to return the calls. Since she has met Mrs. Jones before, a mother very much involved with the school's advisory council, she calls her first. "Hi, Mrs. Jones, this is Mrs. Whitaker from Horace Mann returning your call. What can I do you for?" Mrs. Jones replies, "Oh, hi, Angela, please call me Lily. We don't need to stand on formalities, I feel like I know you so well already. But, I am glad you called. I was just a bit concerned about this portfolio assignment. Miranda expressed to me how much of their grade it represented. And, well, when she has been struggling with the project the past few nights, I became concerned that she was so frustrated and that the project carried so much weight, especially since they really didn't know what exactly you wanted." Angela communicates her appreciation to Lily for alerting her to that point and how she had promised to put together a criteria handout. Unfortunately, it completely slipped her mind, given this first trial run and smoothing out all the other administrative tasks associated with the project. Lily immediately jumps in, saying, "That was another thing, I have always heard you to be a fair teacher, so it surprised me when you made such a new project worth so much of their grade in the class. Seems like there should have been more of a transition period. I also wondered about the more traditional types of assessment. Miranda is such a stellar test taker as you know! It doesn't seem quite fair that their grade pretty much rides on these projects. I see the good points about the project, but while schooling should be about learning to think and solve problems, it is also about gaining the basic content knowledge so they are prepared for college as well, right?" Angela hesitates and decides she needs to regroup, given Mrs. Jones's comments. She politely promises to look into the issue and get back with her the following week.

She glances at the second call slip, wondering what parent complaints it heralds. Given her years in the field, she knows that parent communication usually means one thing: parental dissatisfaction. After she returns the second call, she realizes she was right. Mrs. Franklin is concerned because she feels her son Richard will be at a disadvantage in not having access to the same sophisticated computer graphics and word-processing capabilities as some of the other students in the class. She wants assurances that her son won't be penalized unfairly. After assuring Richard's mother that she will consider her concerns as well as provide some contact information for local public libraries with free computing, Angela hangs up in weary defeat. She groans as she heads out the door. She realizes all will probably look better tomorrow now that the weekend is here.

DISCUSSION TOPICS

1. *Portfolio Assessment*

   a. Distinguish between "process" and "best works" portfolios. Which does the teacher in this case seem to be using? How could her method be revised into the second type of portfolio assessment?

   b. Compare and contrast how the two uses of portfolios relate to the notion of formative versus summative evaluation.

c. An effective tip for using portfolio assessment is to in-volve students in selecting the pieces that will make up the portfolio. How might Angela have allowed for this bit of advice? Create an example for a rubric that would work in this case.

d. Evaluate the strengths and weaknesses of Angela's use of the portfolio exercise. What are its merits? In what ways could it have been more effectively planned? In particular, how might a "scoring rubric" have helped in this case?

2. ***Alternative versus Traditional Assessment***

  a. What makes an assessment "authentic"?

  b. Analyze the issues of reliability and validity of tradi-tional versus alternative assessment.

  c. Evaluate the following argument: "Traditional tests are a poor basis for classroom assessment."

  d. Discuss whether you will use authentic assessment approaches like portfolios and performance exhibi-tions in your own teaching.

3. ***Traditional Tests and Question Types***

  a. Identify the merits of traditional testing.

  b. Describe types of traditional testing Angela might use in her classroom.

  c. Provide some guidelines for constructing traditional tests. What are important ideas to remember when creating true-false, multiple-choice, and matching items?

  d. In what ways is computer assessment much like paper-and-pencil assessment? How can computers help in constructing and administering tests?

4. Fair Testing Practices

a. Identify opportunities for bias in grading.

b. How will you explain your grading system to parents? How can communication with families support students' learning?

c. How can teachers "demystify" the criteria for success on an alternative assessment?

d. Evaluate Angela's explanation of grading policies to students. Were her explanations and standards reasonable?

APPENDIX A

Matrixes

Educator Accomplished Practices Matrix

	1	2	3	4	5	6	7	8	9	10	11	12
Case 1: Another Typical Day		X		X			X		X		X	
Case 2: Resolutions		X			X		X		X		X	
Case 3: Reaching Out		X					X				X	
Case 4: Choices		X					X	X	X		X	
Case 5: Identity Lost		X					X		X			
Case 6: Quick Learners		X	X		X		X		X	X	X	
Case 7: Multiple Intelligences Theory Goes to the Rain Forest	X		X		X		X		X	X		
Case 8: Home and School Culture		X	X		X				X	X	X	X
Case 9: Teaching Jack and Jill	X		X		X		X		X	X		
Case 10: Sink or Swim?	X	X	X		X				X	X	X	
Case 11: The Note		X				X	X		X		X	
Case 12: The Shakespearean Dilemma	X	X	X	X					X	X		
Case 13: The Project		X		X	X		X		X	X	X	
Case 14: Mars in Review				X			X	X	X	X		
Case 15: A Trip Back in Time	X			X	X		X		X	X		
Case 16: Getting Acquainted	X	X					X		X	X		
Case 17: Backfired		X					X		X			X
Case 18: Giving Up							X		X	X		
Case 19: To Belong or Not to Belong		X			X		X		X	X		
Case 20: Interruptions		X					X		X	X	X	
Case 21: Parents' Night		X	X		X	X				X	X	
Case 22: The Rule Breaker		X			X		X		X	X		
Case 23: Purposeful Deliberations	X	X		X	X		X	X				
Case 24: Standardized Testing: A Call to Arms	X	X		X	X					X	X	
Case 25: Meaningful Classroom Assessment	X	X	X	X	X				X	X		X

1. Assessment
2. Communication
3. Continuous Improvement
4. Critical and Creative Thinking
5. Diversity
6. Ethics and Professionalism
7. Human Development and Learning
8. Knowledge and Presentation of Subject Matter
9. Learning Environment
10. Planning
11. Role of Teacher
12. Technology

Praxis II Matrix

	I			II			III			IV	
	A	B	C	A	B	C	A	B	C	A	B
Case 1: Another Day	X		X	X			X				
Case 2: Resolutions	X	X					X	X			
Case 3: Reaching Out	X						X				X
Case 4: Choices	X		X				X				X
Case 5: Identity Lost	X		X								X
Case 6: Quick Learners		X	X	X	X					X	X
Case 7: Multiple Intelligences Goes to the Rain Forest		X					X				
Case 8: Home and School Cultures		X		X				X			X
Case 9: Teaching Jack and Jill		X		X				X			
Case 10: Sink or Swim?		X	X	X							X
Case 11: The Note	X		X		X						
Case 12: The Shakespearean Dilemma	X	X	X	X	X	X	X			X	X
Case 13: The Project	X	X	X	X	X		X		X		
Case 14: Mars in Review	X	X	X	X	X		X		X		
Case 15: A Trip Back in Time	X		X	X	X	X			X		
Case 16: Getting Acquainted	X		X	X			X	X			
Case 17: Backfired				X	X	X					
Case 18: Giving Up		X	X		X						
Case 19: To Belong or Not to Belong	X		X	X							X
Case 20: Interruptions	X		X	X	X		X				
Case 21: Parents' Night				X	X	X	X	X	X	X	X
Case 22: The Rule Breaker	X	X	X	X			X		X		
Case 23: Purposeful Deliberations	X	X	X	X	X	X	X				
Case 24: Standardized Testing: A Call to Arms		X					X				X
Case 25: Meaningful Classroom Assessment		X					X				X

1. Students as Learners
   a. Student Development and Learning Process
   b. Students as Diverse Learners
   c. Student Motivation and the Learning Environment
2. Instruction and Assessment
   a. Instructional Strategies
   b. Planning Instruction
   c. Assessment Strategies
3. Communication Techniques
   a. Basic, effective, verbal and nonverbal communication techniques
   b. Effect of cultural and gender differences on communications in the classroom
   c. Types of questions that can stimulate discussion in different ways for different purposes
4. Profession and Community
   a. The Reflective Practitioner
   b. The Larger Community

APPENDIX B

Outside Readings

Human Development

1. *Cognitive Development: Piaget and Vygotsky (Grades K–2)*

Berk, L. E. (2004). *Development through the lifespan* (3rd ed.). Boston: Allyn & Bacon.

Bigge, M. L., & Shermis, S. S. (2004). *Learning theories for teachers* (6th ed.). Boston: Allyn & Bacon.

Gredler, M. E. (2001). *Learning and instruction* (4th ed.). Upper Saddle River, NJ: Prentice-Hall.

Kozulin, A. (1990). *Vygotsky's psychology: A biography of ideas*. New York: Harvester Wheatsheaf.

Miller, P. H. (1993). *Theories of developmental psychology* (3rd ed.). Belmont, CA: Wadsworth.

Neisser, U. (1967). *Cognitive psychology*. New York: Appleton-Century Crofts.

Piaget, J. (1972). *The psychology of the child*. New York: Basic Books.

Piaget, J. (1990). *The child's conception of the world*. New York: Littlefield Adams.

Piaget, J., Gruber, H. (Ed.), & Voneche, J. J. (Ed.). *The essential Piaget* (100th Anniversary Ed.). New York: Jason Aronson.

Paplia, D. E., & Olds, S. W. (1998). *Human development* (7th ed.). Boston: Mc-Graw-Hill.

Vygotsky, L. (1986). *Thought and language*. Boston: MIT Press.

Vygotsky, L., & Vygotsky, S. (1980). *Mind in society: The development of higher psychological processes*. Cambridge, MA: Harvard University Press.

Vygotsky, L. S. (1978). *Mind in society*. Cambridge, MA: Harvard University Press.

Wertsch, J. V. (1985). *Cultural, communication, and cognition: Vygotskian perspectives*. England: Cambridge University Press.

2. Social Development: Self-Concept, Self-Esteem, and Erikson (Grades 3–5)

Asher, S., & Coie, J. (1990). *Peer rejection in childhood.* New York: Cambridge University Press.

Asher, S. R., Hymel, S., & Renshaw, P. (1984). Loneliness in children. *Child Development, 55,* 1456–1464.

Berk, L. E. (2004). *Development through the lifespan* (3rd ed.). Boston: Allyn & Bacon.

Bierman, K. L. (1986). Process of change during social skills training with preadolescents and its relation to treatment outcomes. *Child Development, 57,* 230–240.

Cowen, E. L., Pederson, A., Babigian, H., Izzo, L. D., & Trost, M. A. (1973). Long-term follow-up of early detected vulnerable children. *Journal of Consulting and Clinical Psychology, 41,* 438–446.

Crick, N. R. (1996). The role of overt aggression, relational aggression, and prosocial behavior in the prediction of children's future social adjustment. *Child Development, 67,* 2317–2327.

Crick, N. R., & Grotpeter, J. K. (1995). Relational aggression, gender, and social-psychological adjustment. *Child Development, 66,* 710–722.

Hymel, S., Wagner, E., & Butler, L. (1990). Reputational bias: View from the peer group. In S. Asher & J. Coie (Eds.), *Peer rejection in childhood* (pp. 156–186). New York: Cambridge University Press.

Kagan, J. (1998). Biology and the child. In W. Damon (Editor-in-Chief) & N. Eisenberg (Vol. Ed.), *Handbook of child psychology: Vol. 3 Social, emotional, and personality development* (5th ed.) (pp. 177–235). New York: Wiley.

Miller, P. H. (1993). *Theories of developmental psychology* (3rd ed.). Belmont, CA: Wadsworth.

Paplia, D. E., & Olds, S. W. (1998). *Human development* (7th ed.). Boston: McGraw-Hill.

Sherif, M., Harvey, O. J., White, B. J., Hood, W. R., & Sherif, C. W. (1961). *Intergroup conflict and cooperation: The Robbers Cave experiment.* Norman: University of Oklahoma Press.

Van Laar, C. (2000). The paradox of low academic achievement but high self-esteem in African American students: An attributional account. *Educational Psychology Review, 12,* 33–61.

Vosk, B., Forehand, R., Parker, J., & Rickard, K. (1982). A multimethod comparison of popular and unpopular children. *Developmental Psychology, 18,* 571–575.

3. Social Development: Bronfenbrenner's Ecological Systems Theory, Divorce

Bronfenbrenner, U., & Crouter, A. C. (1983). The evolution and environmental models in developmental research. In W. Kessen (Ed.), *History, theory and methods,* Volume 1 of P. H. Mussen (Ed.), *Handbook of child psychology* (4th ed.) (pp. 357–414). New York: Wiley.

Bronfenbrenner, U., & Morris, P. A. (1998). The ecology of developmental processes. In R. M. Lerner (Ed.), *Handbook of child psychology* (5th ed., vol. 1), *Theoretical models of human development.* [series ed., W. Damon] (pp. 993–1028). New York: Wiley.

Brown, B. B. (1990). In S. S. Feldman & G. R. Elliott. *At the threshold: The developing adolescent.* Cambridge, MA: Harvard University Press.

Grolnick, W. S., & Slowiaczek, M. L. (1994). Parents' involvement in children's schooling: A multidimensional conceptualization and motivational model. *Child Development, 65,* 237–252.

Henderson, A. T., & Berla, N. (1994). *A new generation of evidence: The family is critical to student achievement.* Columbia, MD: National Committee for Citizens in Education.

Izzo, C. V., Weissberg, R. P., Kasprow, W. J., & Fendrich, M. (1999). A longitudinal assessment of teacher perceptions of parent involvement in children's education and school performance. *American Journal of Community Psychology, 27*(6), 817–839.

Keith, T. Z., Reimers, T. M., Fehrmann, P. G., Pottebaum, S. M., & Aubey, L. W. (1986). Parental involvement, homework, and TV time: Direct and indirect effects on high school achievement. *Journal of Educational Psychology, 78*(5), 373–380.

Lamborn, S. D., Brown, B. B., Mounts, N. S., & Steinberg, L. (1992). Putting school in perspective: The influence of family, peers, extracurricular participation, and part-time work on academic engagement. In F. M. Newmann (Ed.), *Student engagement and achievement in American secondary schools* (pp. 153–181). New York: Teachers College Press.

Marchant, G. J., Paulson, S. E., & Rothlisberg, B. A. (2001). Relations of middle school students' perceptions of family and school contexts with academic achievement. *Psychology in the Schools, 38*(6), 505–519.

Paulson, S. E. (1994). Relations of parenting style and parental involvement with ninth-grade students' achievement. *Journal of Early Adolescence, 14*(2), 250–267.

Rumberger, R. W., Ghatak, R., Poulos, G., Ritter, P. L., & Dornbusch, S. M. (1990). Family influences on dropout behavior in one California high school. *Sociology of Education, 63,* 283–299.

Steinberg, L. (1993). *Adolescence* (3rd ed.). New York: McGraw Hill.

Steinberg, L., Lamborn, S. D., Dornbusch, S. M., & Darling, N. (1992). Impact of parenting practices on adolescent achievement: Authoritative parenting, school involvement, and encouragement to succeed. *Child Development, 63*, 1266–1281.

Trusty, J. (1996). Relationship of parental involvement in teens' career development to teens' attitudes, perceptions and behavior. *Journal of Research and Development in Education, 30*(1), 63–69.

4. *Moral Development: Piaget and Kohlberg (Grades 6–8)*

Baumrind, D. (1966). Effects of authoritative parental control on child behavior. *Child Development, 37(4)*, 887–907.

Baumrind, D. (1968). Authoritarian vs. authoritative parental control. *Adolescence, 3(11)*, 255–272.

Baumrind, D. (1978). Parental disciplinary patterns and social competence in children. *Youth and Society, 9*(3), 239–276.

Berk, L. E. (2004). *Development through the lifespan* (3rd ed.). Boston: Allyn & Bacon.

Gilligan, C. (1982). *In a different voice: Psychological theory and women's development.* Cambridge, MA: Harvard University Press.

Kohlberg, L. (1963). The cognitive-developmental approach to moral education. *Phi Delta Kappan, 56,* 670–677.

Miller, P. H. (1993). *Theories of developmental psychology* (3rd ed.). Belmont, CA: Wadsworth.

Paplia, D. E., & Olds, S. W. (1998). *Human development* (7th ed.). Boston: Mc-Graw-Hill.

Piaget, J. (1965). *The moral judgment of the child.* New York: The Free Press.

Power, F. C., Higgins, A., & Kohlberg, L. (1989). *Lawrence Kohlberg's approach to moral education.* New York: Columbia University Press.

Turiel, E. (1983). *The development of social knowledge: Morality & convention.* New York: Cambridge University Press.

Walker, L. J. (1991). Sex differences in moral reasoning. In W. M. Kurtines & J. L. Gewitz (Eds.), *Handbook of moral behavior and development* (Vol. 2, pp. 333–362). Hillsdale, NJ: Lawrence Erlbaum.

Walker, L. J., & Pitts, R. C. (1998). Naturalistic conceptions of moral maturity. *Developmental Psychology, 34,* 403–419.

Walker, L. J., Pitts, R. C., Henning, K. H., & Matsuba, M. K. (1995). Reasoning about morality and real-life problems. In M. Killen & D. Hart (Eds.), *Morality in everyday life: Developmental perspectives* (pp. 371–407). England: Cambridge University Press.

5. Social/Identity Development: Erikson and Marcia (Grades 9–12)

Baumrind, D. (1965). Parental control and parental love. *Children, 12,* 230–234.

Baumrind, D. (1966). Effects of authoritative parental control on child behavior. *Child Development, 37*(4), 887–907.

Baumrind, D. (1968). Authoritarian vs. authoritative parental control. *Adolescence, 3*(11), 255–272.

Baumrind, D. (1983). Three commentaries on teenage sexuality. *American Psychologist, 36,* 528–529 and 530–531; *37*(12), 1402–1403.

Baumrind, D. (1991). The influence of parenting style on adolescent competence and substance abuse. *Journal of Early Adolescence, 11*(1), 56–95.

Baumrind, D. (1991). Parenting styles and adolescent development. In J. Brooks-Gunn, R. Lerner & A. C. Petersen (Eds.), *The encyclopedia on adolescence* (pp. 746–758). New York: Garland.

Baumrind, D. (1992). Adolescent exploratory behavior: Precursors and consequences. In L. P. Lipsitt & L. L. Mitnick (Eds.), *Self-regulation and risk-taking* (pp. 109–142). Norwood, NJ: Ablex.

Berk, L. E. (2004). *Development through the lifespan* (3rd ed.). Boston: Allyn & Bacon.

Bronfenbrenner, U. (1977). Toward an experimental ecology of human development. *American Psychologist, 32,* 513–531.

Bronfenbrenner, U., & Ceci, S. J. (1994). Nature-nurture reconceptualized: A bio-ecological model. *Psychological Review, 101*(4), 568–586.

Fischman, W., Solomon, B., Greenspan, D., & Gardner, H. (2004). *Making good: How young people cope with moral dilemmas at work.* Cambridge, MA: Harvard University Press. Translated into Spanish and Korean.

Kohlberg, L. (1963). The development of children's orientations toward moral order: Sequence in the development of moral thought. *Vita Humana, 6,* 11–13.

Miller, P. H. (1993). *Theories of developmental psychology* (3rd ed.). Belmont, CA: Wadsworth.

Paplia, D. E., & Olds, S. W. (1998). *Human development* (7th ed.). Boston: McGraw-Hill.

Santrock, J. (1996). *Child development.* Dubuque, IA: Brown and Benchmark.

Individual Differences and Diversity

6. *Intelligence: IQ, Origins, Heredity vs. Environment, Sternberg, Gardner, Ability Grouping, Gifted & Instruction*

Gardner, H. (1991). *The unschooled mind: How children think and how schools should teach*. New York: Basic Books.

Gardner, H. (2000). *The disciplined mind: Beyond facts and standardized tests, the K–12 education that every child deserves*. New York: Penguin Putnam.

Gardner, H., with the collaboration of Laskin, E. (1995). *Leading minds: An anatomy of leadership*. New York: Basic Books. Basic Books Paperback with a new introduction, 1996.

Guilford, J. P. (1967). *The nature of human intelligence*. New York: McGraw-Hill.

Guilford, J. P. (1982). Cognitive psychology's ambiguities: Some suggested remedies. *Psychological Review, 89,* 48–59.

Guilford, J. P., & Hoepfner, R. (1971). *The analysis of intelligence*. New York: McGraw-Hill.

Meeker, M. N. (1969). *The structure of intellect*. Columbus, OH: Merrill.

Sternberg, R. J. (1977). *Intelligence, information processing, and analogical reasoning*. Hillsdale, NJ: Erlbaum.

Sternberg, R. J. (1983). Criteria for intellectual skills training. *Educational Researcher, 12,* 6–12.

Sternberg, R. J. (1985). *Beyond IQ*. New York: Cambridge University Press.

Sternberg, R. J. (1997). What does it mean to be smart? *Educational Leadership, 5,* 20–24.

Sternberg, R. J. (1998). Abilities are forms of developing expertise. *Educational Researcher, 27,* 11–20.

Sternberg, R. J. (1999). Successful intelligence: Finding a balance. *Trends in Cognitive Sciences, 3,* 436–442.

Sternberg, R. J. (1999). The theory of successful intelligence. *Review of General Psychology, 3,* 292–316.

Williams, W. M., Blythe, T., White, N., Li, J., Sternberg, R. J., & Gardner, H. (1996). *Practical intelligence for school*. New York: HarperCollins College.

7. *Intelligence: Multiple Intelligence, Sternberg, Gardner, Controversies (Grades 3–5)*

Cambell, L., Cambell, B., & Dickinson, D. (2004). *Teaching and learning through multiple intelligences* (3rd ed.). Boston: Allyn & Bacon.

Gardner, H. (1993). *Multiple intelligences: The theory in practice*. New York: Basic Books.

Gardner, H. (1997). *Extraordinary minds: Portraits of exceptional individuals and an examination of our extraordinariness.* New York: Basic Books.

Gardner, H. (1999). *Intelligence reframed.* New York: Basic Books.

Gardner, H. (1999). *Intelligence reframed: Multiple intelligences for the 21st century.* New York: Basic Books.

Gardner, H., Kornhaber, M., & Wake, W. (1996). *Intelligence: Multiple perspectives.* Fort Worth, TX: Harcourt Brace.

Goleman, D. (1995). *Emotional intelligence: Why it can matter more than IQ.* New York: Bantam Books.

Kornhaber, M., Ferros, E., & Veenema, S. (2004). *Multiple intelligences: Best ideas from research and practice.* Boston: Allyn & Bacon.

Steinberg, R. J. (Ed.). (1994). *Encyclopedia of human intelligence.* New York: Macmillan.

Sternberg, R. J. (1996). Myths, countermyths, and truths about human intelligence. *Educational Researcher, 25*(2), 11–16.

Sternberg, R. J. (1996). What should we ask about intelligence? *American Scholar, 65*(2), 205–217.

Sternberg, R. J., Wagner, R. K., Williams, W. M., & Horvath, J. A. (1995). Testing common sense. *American Psychologist, 50*(11), 912–927.

Weber, E. (2005). *MI strategies in the classroom and beyond: Using roundtable learning.* Boston: Allyn & Bacon.

8. Culture and Ethnicity: SES, Discrimination, Bilingualism, Multiculturalism (Grades 3–5)

Abi-Nader, J. (1991). Creating a vision of the future: Strategies for motivating minority students. *Phi Delta Kappan, 72,* 546–549.

Baumrind, D. (1972). An exploratory study of socialization effects on black children: Some black-white comparisons. *Child Development, 43*(1), 261–267.

Björkqvist, K. (1994). Sex differences in physical, verbal, and indirect aggression: A review of recent research. *Sex Roles, 30,* 177–188.

Björkqvist, K., Lagerspetz, K., & Kaukiainen, A. (1992). Do girls manipulate and boys fight? Developmental trends in regard to direct and indirect aggression. *Aggressive Behavior, 18,* 117–127.

Brown, B. (1990). Cliques and crowds. In L. Steinberg (Ed.), *Adolescence* (pp. 163–164). New York: McGraw-Hill Companies.

Bowman, B. (1992). *Cultural diversity and academic achievement.* (Excerpt from monograph.) Oak Brook, IL: North Central Regional Educational Laboratory.

Campbell, F. A., & Ramey, C. T. (1995). Cognitive and school outcomes for high-risk African American students at middle adolescence: Positive effects of early intervention. *American Association Research Journal 32 (4),* 743–772.

DiMaggio, P. (1997). Culture and cognition. *Annual Review of Sociology, 23,* 263–288.

Garcia, E. E. (2001). *Hispanic education in the United States.* Cumnor Hill, Oxford, England: Rowman & Littlefield.

Gay, G. (1994). *Synthesis of scholarship in multicultural education.* (Monograph.) Oak Brook, IL: North Central Regional Educational Laboratory.

Kindermann, T. A., & Valsiner, J. (1989). Research strategies in culture-inclusive developmental psychology. In J. Valsiner (Ed.), *Child development in cultural context* (pp. 13–50). Göttingen/Toronto: Hogrefe.

Lindblad-Goldberg, M. (1989). Successful minority single-parent families. In L. Combrink-Graham (Ed.), *Children in family contexts.* New York: Guilford.

Rio, A. T., Santisteban, D. A., & Szapocznik, J. (1991). Juvenile delinquency among Hispanics: The role of the family in prevention and treatment. In M. Sotomayor (Ed.), *Empowering Hispanic families: A critical issue for the 90s.* Milwaukee: Family Service America.

Schorr, L. B. (1988). *Within our reach: Breaking the cycle of disadvantage.* New York: Doubleday.

Vasquez, J. A. (1990). Teaching to the distinctive traits of minority students. *The Clearing House, 63,* 299–304.

9. Gender Roles: Biological, Socialization, Stereotyping, Differences in Academic Domains, Gender Sensitive Teaching (Grades 9–12)

Beall, A. E., & Sternberg, R. J. (Eds.). (1993). *The psychology of gender.* New York: Guilford.

Brown, B. (1990). Cliques and crowds. In L. Steinberg (Ed.), *Adolescence* (pp. 163–164). New York: McGraw-Hill.

Brown, B. (1990). Peer groups and peer culture. In S. S. Feldman & G. R. Elliott (Eds.), *At the threshold: The developing adolescent* (pp. 171–196). Cambridge, MA: Harvard University Press.

Cotterell, J. (1996). *Social networks and social influences in adolescence.* London: Routledge.

Crick, N. R., & Grotpeter, J .K. (1995). Relational aggression, gender, and social-psychological adjustment. *Child Development, 66,* 710–722.

Gurian, M., & Henley, P. (2001). *Boys and girls learn differently!: A guide for teachers and parents.* San Francisco, CA: Jossey-Bass.

Kindermann, T. A. (1996). Strategies for the study of individual development within naturally-existing peer groups. *Social Development, 5,* 158–173.

Kindermann, T. A. (1998). Children's development within peer groups: Using composite social maps to identify networks and to study their influences. In W. Damon (Ed.), W. M. Bukowski & A. H. N. Cillessen (Series Eds.). *New directions in child development* (Vol. 80, Summer). Sociometry then and now: Building on six decades of measuring children's experiences within the peer group. San Francisco, CA: Jossey-Bass.

Kindermann, T. A. (2003). Development of children's social relationships. In J. Valsiner & K. Connolly (Eds.), *Handbook of developmental psychology* (pp. 407–430). Thousand Oaks, CA: Sage.

Kindermann, T. A., McCollam, T. L., & Gibson, E. Jr. (1996). Peer group influences on children's developing school motivation. In K. Wentzel & J. Juvonon (Eds.), *Social motivation: Understanding children's school adjustment.* (279–312). Newbury Park, CA: Sage.

Lagerspetz, K. M., Bjorkqvist, K., & Peltonen, T. (1988). Is indirect aggression typical of females? Gender differences in aggressiveness in 11- to 12-year-old children. *Aggressive Behavior, 14,* 403–414.

Maher, F. A., & Ward, J. V. (2002). *Gender and teaching.* Mahwah, NJ: Erlbaum.

Paquette, J., & Underwood, M. (1999). Gender differences in young adolescents' experiences of peer victimization: Social and physical aggression. *Merrill-Palmer Quarterly, 45,* 242–265.

Sage, N. A., & Kindermann, T. A. (1999). Peer networks, behavior contingencies, and children's engagement in the classroom. *Merrill-Palmer Quarterly 454*(1), 143–171.

Tittle, C. (1986). Gender research and education. *American Psychologist, 41*(10), 1161–1168.

Witt, S. D. (1997). Parental influence on children's socialization to gender roles. *Adolescence, 32,* 253–259.

10. *Exceptionalities: Categories: ADHD, Learning Disabilities, IDEA (Grades 6–8)*

Bender, W. N. (2004). *Learning disabilities: Characteristics, identification, and teaching strategies* (5th ed.). Boston: Allyn & Bacon.

Brown, A., & Campione, J. (1986). Psychological theory and the study of learning disabilities. *American Psychologist, 14*(10), 1059–1068.

Choate, J. S. (Ed.). (2003). *Successful inclusive teaching: Proven ways to detect and correct special needs* (4th ed.). Boston: Allyn & Bacon.

Dolgins, J., Myers, M., Flynn, P., & Moore, J. (1986). How do we help the learning disabled? In F. Linder & J. McMillan (Eds.). *Educational psychology: Annual editions 1986/87* (pp. 174–179). Guilford, CT: Dushkin.

Feldhusen, J. (1989). Synthesis of research on gifted youth. *Educational Leadership, 46*(6), 6–11.

Huitt, K. (1999). *Teaching dyslexic students.* Paper prepared for Psychological Foundations of Learning. Atlanta, GA: Oglethorpe University.

Hunt, N., & Marshall, K. (2002). *Exceptional children and youth* (3rd ed.). Boston: Houghton Mifflin.

Jaksa, P. (1998). *Fact sheet on attention deficit hyperactivity disorder (ADHD/ADD).* Highland Park, IL: National Attention Deficit Disorder Association.

Kirk, S. A., Gallagher, J. J., & Anastasiow, N. J. (2003). *Educating exceptional children* (10th ed.). Boston: Houghton Mifflin.

Knight, C., Peterson, R., & McGuire, B. (1982). Cooperative learning: A new approach to an old idea. *Teaching Exceptional Children, 233–238.*

Lerner, J. W. (2003). *Learning disabilities: Theories, diagnosis, and teaching strategies* (9th ed.). Boston: Houghton Mifflin.

Passow, A. (1981). The nature of giftedness and talent. *Gifted Child Quarterly* (Winter), 5–10.

Salend, S. (1984). Factors contributing to the development of successful mainstreaming programs. *Exceptional Children,* (February), 409–416.

Sternberg, R. J. (1983). Criteria for intellectual skills training. *Educational Researcher, 12,* 6–12.

Sternberg, R. J. (1997). What does it mean to be smart? *Educational Leadership, 5,* 20–24.

Learning Theories

11. Classical Conditioning (Grades 6–8)

Bacon, E. (1989). Guidelines for implementing a classroom reward system. *Academic Therapy, 25,* 183–192.

Bigge, M. L., & Shermis, S. S. (2004). *Learning theories for teachers* (6th ed.). Boston: Allyn & Bacon.

Bouton, M. E., Nelson, J. B., & Rosas, J. M. (1999). Stimulus generalization, context change, and forgetting. *Psychological Bulletin, 125,* 171–186.

Emmer, E., Evertson, C., & Anderson, L. (1980). Effective classroom management at the beginning of the school year. *The Elementary School Journal, 80*(5), 219–231.

Estes, W. (1989). Learning theory. In A. Lesgold & R. Glaser (Eds.), *Handbook of research on teaching* (pp. 1–49). Hillsdale, NJ: Erlbaum.

Gredler, M. E. (2001). *Learning and instruction* (4th ed.). Upper Saddle River, NJ: Prentice-Hall.

Hollis, K. L. (1997). Contemporary research on Pavlovian conditioning: A "new" functional analysis. *American Psychologist, 52,* 956–965.

Horowitz, F. D. (1992). John B. Watson's legacy: Learning and environment. *Developmental Psychology, 28,* 360–367.

Kratochwill, T. R., & Bijou, S. W. (1987). The impact of behaviorism on educational psychology. In J. A. Glover & R. R. Ronning (Eds.), *Historical foundations of educational psychology* (pp. 131–157). New York: Plenum.

Leahey, T., & Harris, R. (1997). *Learning and cognition* (4th ed.). Upper Saddle River, NJ: Prentice-Hall.

Schunk, D. H. (2004). *Learning theories: An educational perspective* (4th ed.). Upper Saddle River, NJ: Prentice-Hall.

Skinner, B. F. (1950). Are theories of learning necessary? *Psychological Review, 57*(4), 193–216.

Skinner, B. F. (1954). The science of learning and the art of teaching. *Harvard Educational Review, 24*(2), 86–97.

Skinner, B. F. (1957). *Verbal learning.* New York: Appleton-Century-Crofts.

Tauber, R. T. (1990). Classical conditioning: Eliciting the right response. *NASSP Bulletin, 74*(5), 90–92.

Todes, D. P. (1997). From the machine to the ghost within: Pavlov's transition from digestive physiology to conditioned reflexes. *Commemorating Pavlov's work: American Psychologist, 52*(9), 947–955.

Windholdz, G. (1997). Ivan P. Pavlov: An overview of his life and psychological work. *American Psychologist, 52,* 941–946.

12. Operant Conditioning (Grades 9–12)

Bigge, M. L., & Shermis, S. S. (2004). *Learning theories for teachers* (6th ed.). Boston: Allyn & Bacon.

Fabes, R. (1989). Effects of rewards on children's prosocial motivation: A socialization study. *Developmental Psychology, 25,* 509–515.

Gredler, M. E. (2001). *Learning and instruction* (4th ed.). Upper Saddle River, NJ: Prentice-Hall.

Kazdin, A., & Bootzin, R. (1972). The token economy: An evaluative review. *Journal of Applied Behavior Analysis, 5,* 359–360.

Kohn, A. (1993). Rewards verses learning: A response to Paul Chance. *Phi Delta Kappan, 74,* 783–787.

Kohn, A. (1996). By all available means: Cameron and Pierce's defense of extrinsic motivators. *Review of Educational Research, 66,* 1–4.

Leahey, T., & Harris, R. (1997). *Learning and cognition* (4th ed.). Upper Saddle River, NJ: Prentice-Hall.

Lepper, M., Greene, D., & Nisbett, R. (1973). Undermining children's intrinsic interest with extrinsic rewards. *Journal of Personality and Social Psychology, 28,* 129–137.

Lepper, M., & Greene, D. (1978). *The hidden cost of rewards.* Hillsdale, NJ: Erlbaum.

Marshall, H. (1995). Beyond "I like the way . . . " *Young Children, 50,* 26–28.

Matthews, D. (1991). The effects of school environment on intrinsic motivation of middle-school children. *Journal of Humanistic Education and Development, 30,* 30–36.

Schunk, D. H. (2004). *Learning theories: An educational perspective* (4th ed.). Upper Saddle River, NJ: Prentice-Hall.

Skinner, B. F. (1950). Are theories of learning necessary? *Psychological Review, 57*(4), 193–216.

Skinner, B. F. (1954). The science of learning and the art of teaching. *Harvard Educational Review, 24*(2), 86–97.

Skinner, B. F. (1957). *Verbal learning.* New York: Appleton-Century-Crofts.

13. Social Cognitive Theory: Reciprocal Determinism and Observational Learning (Grades K–2)

Bandura, A. (1977). *Social learning theory.* Englewood Cliffs, NJ: Prentice-Hall.

Bandura, A. (1986). *Social foundations of thought and action: A social cognitive theory.* Englewood Cliffs, NJ: Prentice-Hall.

Bandura, A. (1994). Self-efficacy. In V. S. Ramachaudran (Ed.), *Encyclopedia of human behavior* (Vol. 4) (pp. 71–81). New York: Academic Press

Bandura, A. (1997). *Self-efficacy: The exercise of control.* New York: Freeman.

Bandura, A. (1999). A social cognitive theory of personality. In L. Pervin & O. John (Eds.), *Handbook of personality* (2nd ed.) (pp. 154–196). New York: Guilford.

Bandura, A. (2002). Social cognitive theory in cultural context. *Journal of Applied Psychology: An International Review, 51,* 269–290.

Bigge, M. L., & Shermis, S. S. (2004). *Learning theories for teachers* (6th ed.). Boston: Allyn & Bacon.

Bussey, K., & Bandura, A. (1999). Social cognitive theory of gender development and differentiation. *Psychological Review, 106,* 676–713.

Gagne, E. D., Yekovich, C. W., & Yekovich, F. R. (1993). *The cognitive psychology of school learning.* New York: Harper Collins.

Gredler, M. E. (2001). *Learning and instruction* (4th ed.). Upper Saddle River, NJ: Prentice-Hall.

Leahey, T., & Harris, R. (1997). *Learning and cognition* (4th ed.). Upper Saddle River, NJ: Prentice-Hall.

Pajares, F. (1997). Current directions in self-efficacy research. In M. Maehr & P. R. Pintrich (Eds.), *Advances in motivation and achievement* (Vol. 10) (pp. 1–49). Greenwich, CT: JAI Press.

Pajares, F. (1996). Self-efficacy beliefs in academic settings. *Review of Educational Research, 66*(4), 543–578.

Palincsar, S. (1998). Social constructivist perspectives on teaching and learning. *Annual Reviews in Psychology, 49,* 345–375.

Schunk, D. H. (2004). *Learning theories: An educational perspective* (4th ed.). Upper Saddle River, NJ: Prentice-Hall.

14. Cognitive Theories: Information Processing and Metacognition (Grades 6–8)

Derry, S. (1988/89, December-January). Putting learning strategies to work. *Educational Leadership,* 4–10.

Derry, S. J. (1992). Beyond symbolic processing: Expanding horizons for educational psychology. *Journal of Educational Psychology, 84,* 413–419.

Eisner, E. (1988, Spring). The celebration of thinking. *National Forum,* 30–33.

Gagne, E. D., Yekovich, C. W., & Yekovich, F. R. (1993). *The cognitive psychology of school learning.* New York: Harper Collins.

Goffin, S., & Tull, C. (1985, March). Problem solving: Encouraging active learning. *Young Children,* 28–32.

Goleman, D. (1995, May 2). Biologists find site of working memory. *New York Times,* C1, C9.

Gredler, M. E. (2001). *Learning and instruction* (4th ed.). Upper Saddle River, NJ: Prentice-Hall.

Isenberg, J., & Jacobs, J. (1981, May/June). Classification: Something to think about. *Childhood Education,* 284–288.

Johnson, D., Pittelman, S., & Heimlich, J. (1986, April). Semantic mapping. *The Reading Teacher,* 779–783.

Jones, B. (1986, April). Quality and equality through cognitive instruction. *Educational Leadership,* 4–11.

Leahey, T., & Harris, R. (1997). *Learning and cognition* (4th ed.). Upper Saddle River, NJ: Prentice-Hall.

Martin, D. (1984, November). Infusing cognitive strategies into teacher preparation programs. *Educational Leadership,* 68–72.

Mayer, R. E. (1996). Learners as information processors: Legacies and limitations of educational psychology's second metaphor. *Educational Psychologist, 31,* 151–161.

Neimark, J. (1995, January/February). It's magical! It's malleable! It's . . . memory. *Psychology Today,* 44–45, 80, 85.

Schunk, D. H. (2004). *Learning theories: An educational perspective* (4th ed.). Upper Saddle River, NJ: Prentice-Hall.

Sywlester, R. (1985, April). Research on memory: Major discoveries, major educational challenges. *Educational Leadership,* 69–75.

15. Social Constructivism: Situated Cognition, Tutoring, Cooperative Learning, Authentic Instruction, Problem-Based Learning (Grades 9–12)

Abdullah, M. H. (1998). *Problem-based learning in language instruction: A constructivist model.* Bloomington, IN: ERIC Clearinghouse on Reading, English, and Communication.

Cobb, P. (1994). Where is the mind? Constructivist and sociocultural perspectives on mathematical development. *Educational Researcher, 23*(7), 13–20.

Cobb, P., & Yackel, R. (1996). Constructivist, emergent, and sociocultural perspectives in the context of developmental research. *Educational Psychologist, 31,* 175–190.

Gagne, E. D., Yekovich, C. W., & Yekovich, F. R. (1993). *The cognitive psychology of school learning.* New York: Harper Collins.

Harley, S. (1993). Situated learning and classroom instruction. *Educational Technology, 33*(3), 46–50.

Kumar, D., & Voldrich, J. F. (1994). Situated cognition in second grade science: Literature books for authentic contexts. *Journal of Elementary Science Education, 6*(2), 1–10.

Lave, J. (1988). *Cognition in practice: Mind, mathematics and culture in everyday life.* Cambridge, MA: Cambridge University Press.

Leahey, T., & Harris, R. (1997). *Learning and cognition* (4th ed.). Upper Saddle River, NJ: Prentice-Hall.

McLellan, H. (1994). Situated learning: Continuing the conversation. *Educational Technology, 34*(8), 7–8.

Moore, J. L., Lin, X., Schwartz, D. L., Petrosino, A., Hickey, D. T., Campbell, O., Hmelo, C., & The Cognition and Technology Group at Vanderbilt. (1994). The relationship between situated cognition and anchored instruction: A response to Steven Tripp. *Educational Technology, 34*(8), 28–31.

Prawat, R. S. (1996). Constructivism, modern and postmodern. *Educational Psychologist, 31,* 215–225.

Schunk, D. H. (2004). *Learning theories: An educational perspective* (4th ed.). Upper Saddle River, NJ: Prentice-Hall.

Slavin, R. E. (1995). *Cooperative learning: Theory, research, and practice* (2nd ed.). Boston: Allyn & Bacon.

Schofield, J. W., Davidson, A., Stocks, J. E., and Futoran, G. (1997). The Internet in school: A case study of educator demand and its precursors. In S. Kiesler (Ed.), *Culture of the Internet* (pp. 361–381). Mahwah, NJ: Lawrence Erlbaum Associates.

Wells, A. (1996). Situated action, symbol systems and universal computation. *Minds and Machines, 6,* 33–46.

16. *Applications of Operant Conditioning: Schedules, Peer Tutoring, Contracts, Punishments (Grades 3–5)*

Bacon, E. (1989). Guidelines for implementing a classroom reward system. *Academic Therapy, 25,* 183–192.

Bigge, M. L., & Shermis, S. S. (2004). *Learning theories for teachers* (6th ed.). Boston: Allyn & Bacon.

Gredler, M. E. (2001). *Learning and instruction* (4th ed.). Upper Saddle River, NJ: Prentice-Hall.

Kazdin, A., & Bootzin, R. (1972). The token economy: An evaluative review. *Journal of Applied Behavior Analysis, 5,* 359–360.

Kohn, A. (1993). Rewards versus learning: A response to Paul Chance. *Phi Delta Kappan, 74,* 783–787.

Kohn, A. (1996). By all available means: Cameron and Pierce's defense of extrinsic motivators. *Review of Educational Research, 66,* 1–4.

Leahey, T., & Harris, R. (1997). *Learning and cognition* (4th ed.). Upper Saddle River, NJ: Prentice-Hall.

McDaniel, T. (1987, May). Practicing positive reinforcement: Ten behavior management techniques. *The Clearing House,* 389–392.

Roetter, P. (1987, April/May). The positive approach in the classroom. *The High School Journal,* 196–202.

Schunk, D. H. (2004). *Learning theories: An educational perspective* (4th ed.). Upper Saddle River, NJ: Prentice-Hall.

Skinner, B. F. (1950). Are theories of learning necessary? *Psychological Review, 57*(4), 193–216.

Skinner, B. F. (1953). *Science and human behavior.* New York: Macmillan.

Skinner, B. F. (1954). The science of learning and the art of teaching. *Harvard Educational Review, 24*(2), 86–97.

Skinner, B. F. (1957). *Verbal learning.* New York: Appleton-Century-Crofts.

Skinner, B. F. (1968). *The technology of teaching.* New York: Appleton-Century-Crofts.

Skinner, B. F. (1971). *Beyond freedom and dignity.* New York: Knopf.

Skinner, B. F. (1987). Whatever happened to psychology as the science of behavior? *American Psychologist, 42,* 780–786.

Motivation

17. Extrinsic and Intrinsic Motivation (Grades 3–5)

Brandt, R. (1995). Punished by rewards? A conversation with Alfie Kohn. *Educational Leadership, 53,* 13–16.

Chance, P. (1992). The rewards of learning. *Phi Delta Kappan, 73,* 200–207.

Deci, E. (1971). Effects of externally mediated rewards on intrinsic motivation. *Journal of Personality and Social Psychology, 18,* 105–115.

Deci, E., & Ryan, R. (1985). *Intrinsic motivation and self-determination in human behavior.* New York: Plenum.

Dweck, C. (2000). *Essays in social psychology, self-theories: Their role in motivation, personality, and development.* Lillington, NC: Taylor and Francis.

Eskeles-Gottfried, A., Fleming, J., & Gottfried, A. (1994). Role of parental motivational practices in children's academic intrinsic motivation and achievement. *Journal of Educational Psychology, 86,* 104–113.

Fabes, R. (1989). Effects of rewards on children's prosocial motivation: A socialization study. *Developmental Psychology, 25,* 509–515.

Graham S., & Weiner, B. (1996). Theories and principles of motivation. In D. Berliner & R. Calfee (Eds.), *Handbook of educational psychology* (pp. 63–84). New York: Macmillan.

Kindermann, T. A. (1993). Natural peer groups as contexts for individual development: The case of children's motivation in school. *Developmental Psychology, 29,* 970–977.

Kohn, A. (1996). By all available means: Cameron and Pierce's defense of extrinsic motivators. *Review of Educational Research, 66,* 1–4.

Leahey, T., & Harris, R. (1997). *Learning and cognition* (4th ed.). Upper Saddle River, NJ: Prentice-Hall.

Maehr, M. L., & Pintrich, P. R. (1997). *Advances in motivation and achievement, Vol. 10.* Greenwich, CT: JAI Press.

Matthews, D. (1991). The effects of school environment on intrinsic motivation of middle-school children. *Journal of Humanistic Education and Development, 30,* 30–36.

Meyer, M. R., & Middleton, J. A. (1993). Affect and motivation in secondary mathematics. In A. E. Woolfolk (Ed.), *Readings and cases in educational psychology* (pp. 286–291). Needham Heights, MA: Allyn & Bacon.

Middleton, J. (1995). A study of intrinsic motivation in the mathematics classroom: A personal constructs approach. *Journal for Research in Mathematics Education, 26,* 254–279.

Peterson, R. (1992). *Life in a crowded place.* Portsmouth, NH: Heinemann.

Stipek, D. J. (1998). *Motivation to learn: From theory to practice* (3rd ed.). Boston: Allyn & Bacon.

Schunk, D. H. (2004). *Learning theories: An educational perspective* (4th ed.). Upper Saddle River, NJ: Prentice-Hall.

18. Attributions, Self-Efficacy, Self-Regulation, Goal Theory (Grades 9–12)

Bandura, A. (1994). Self-efficacy. In V. S. Ramachaudran (Ed.), *Encyclopedia of human behavior* (Vol. 4) (pp. 71–81). New York: Academic Press.

Brandt, R. (1995). Punished by rewards? A conversation with Alfie Kohn. *Educational Leadership, 53,* 13–16.

Chance, P. (1992). The rewards of learning. *Phi Delta Kappan, 73,* 200–207.

Deci, E. (1971). Effects of externally mediated rewards on intrinsic motivation. *Journal of Personality and Social Psychology, 18,* 105–115.

Deci, E., & Ryan, R. (1985). *Intrinsic motivation and self-determination in human behavior.* New York: Plenum.

Dweck, C. (2000). *Essays in social psychology, self-theories: Their role in motivation, personality, and development.* Lillington, NC: Taylor and Francis.

Graham, S., & Weiner, B. (1996). Theories and principles of motivation. In D. Berliner & R. Calfee (Eds.), *Handbook of educational psychology* (pp. 63–84). New York: Macmillan.

Gredler, M. E. (2001). *Learning and instruction* (4th ed.). Upper Saddle River, NJ: Prentice-Hall.

Maehr, M. L., & Pintrich, P. R. (1997). *Advances in motivation and achievement, Vol. 10.* Greenwich, CT: JAI Press.

Ryan, R., & Deci, E. (1996). When paradigms clash: Comments on Cameron and Pierce's claim that rewards do not undermine intrinsic motivation. *Review of Educational Research, 66,* 33–38.

Schunk, D. H. (2004). *Learning theories: An educational perspective* (4th ed.). Upper Saddle River, NJ: Prentice-Hall.

Stipek, D. J. (1998). *Motivation to learn: From theory to practice* (3rd ed.). Boston: Allyn & Bacon.

Strong, R., Silver, H., & Robinson, A. (1995). What do students want (and what really motivates them)? *Educational Leadership, 53,* 8–12.

Valas, S., & Sovik, N. (1993). Variables affecting students' intrinsic motivation for school mathematics: Two empirical studies based on Deci and Ryan's theory on motivation. *Learning and Instruction, 3,* 281–298.

19. Maslow's Need Hierarchy (Grades 6–8)

Aspy, D., & Roebuck, F. (1977). *Kid's don't learn from people they don't like.* Amherst, MA: Human Resources Development Press.

Beane, J. (1990). Affective dimensions of effective middle schools. *Educational Horizons, 68(2),* 109–112.

Benninga, J., & Crum, R. (1982, January/February). "Acting out" for social understanding. *Childhood Education,* 144–148.

Combs, A. (1981, February). Humanistic education: Too tender for a tough world? *Phi Delta Kappan,* 446–449.

DeCarvalho, R. J. (1991). The humanistic paradigm in education. *The Humanistic Psychologist, 19*(1), 88–104.

Edwords, F. (1989). *What is humanism?* Amherst, NY: American Humanist Association.

Gianconia, R., & Hedges, L. (1982). Identifying features of effective open education. *Review of Educational Research, 52*(4), 579–602.

Gogineni, B. (2000). Humanism in the twenty-first century. *The Humanist, 60*(6), 27–31.

Graham, S., & Weiner, B. (1996). Theories and principles of motivation. In D. Berliner & R. Calfee (Eds.), *Handbook of educational psychology* (pp. 63–84). New York: Macmillan.

Huitt, W. (1995). *An overview of a systems model of human behavior.* Valdosta, GA: Valdosta State University.

Kohn, A. (1991, March). Caring kids: The role of the schools. *Phi Delta Kappan,* 496–506.

Kurtz, P. (2000). *Humanist manifesto 2000: A call for a new planetary humanism.* Amherst, NY: Prometheus Books.

Maehr, M. L., & Pintrich, P. R. (1997). *Advances in motivation and achievement, Vol. 10.* Greenwich, CT: JAI Press.

Rogers, C., & Freiberg, H. J. (1994). *Freedom to learn* (3rd ed.). New York: Macmillan/Merrill.

Staats, A. (1987, November). Humanistic volition versus behavioristic determinism: Disunified psychology's schism problem and its solution. *American Psychologist,* 1030–1032.

Stipek, D. J. (1998). *Motivation to learn: From theory to practice* (3rd ed.). Boston: Allyn & Bacon.

Classroom Management

20. Handling Problem Behaviors: Behavioral Approaches (Grades K–2)

Bacon, E. (1989). Guidelines for implementing a classroom reward system. *Academic Therapy, 25,* 183–192.

Bloom, B. (1986). What we're learning about teaching and learning: A summary of recent research. *Principal, 66*(2), 6–10.

Bredekamp, S. (1988, January). NAEYC position statement on developmentally appropriate practice in the primary grades, serving 5- through 8-year-olds. *Young Children,* 64–84.

Brophy, J. (1986). Teacher influences on student achievement. *American Psychologist, 41*(10), 1069–1077.

Brophy, J., & Good, T. (1986). Teacher behavior and student achievement. In M. Wittrock (Ed.). *Handbook of research on teaching* (3rd ed.) (pp. 328–370). New York: Macmillan.

Caldwell, J., Huitt, W., & Graeber, A. (1982). Time spent in learning: Implications from research. *The Elementary School Journal, 82*(5), 470–480.

Carroll, J. (1963). A model of school learning. *Teachers College Record, 64,* 723–733.

Charles, C. M. (2005). *Building classroom discipline* (8th ed.). Boston: Allyn & Bacon.

Driscoll, M. (1986). Effective teaching. *Arithmetic Teacher, 33*(9), 19 & 48.

Hunter, M. (1979). Teaching is decision making. *Educational Leadership, 37*(1), 62–67.

McDaniel, T. (1987, May). Practicing positive reinforcement: Ten behavior management techniques. *The Clearing House,* 389–392.

Roetter, P. (1987, April/May). The positive approach in the classroom. *The High School Journal,* 196–202.

Rosenshine, B., & Stevens, R. (1986). Teaching functions. In M. Wittrock (Ed.). *Handbook of research on teaching* (3rd ed.) (pp. 3–33). New York: Macmillan.

Skinner, B. F. (1987). Whatever happened to psychology as the science of behavior? *American Psychologist, 42,* 780–786.

Stallings, J., & Stipek, D. (1986). Research on early childhood and elementary school teaching programs. In M. Wittrock (Ed.). *Handbook of research on teaching* (3rd ed.) (pp. 727–753). New York: Macmillan.

Walberg, H. (1988, March). Synthesis of research on time and learning. *Educational Leadership,* 76–80.

21. *Effective Communication with Students' Parents: Parent Involvement, Conference (Grades 6–8)*

Ames, C., de Stefano, L., Watkins, T., & Sheldon, S. (1995). *Teachers' school-to-home communications and parent involvement: The role of parent perceptions and beliefs* (Report No. 28). East Lansing, MI: Center on Families, Communities, Schools, and Children's Learning, Michigan State University. (ERIC Document Service No. ED383451).

Ames, C., Khoju, M., & Watkins, T. (1993). *Parent involvement: The relationship between school-to-home communication and parents' perceptions and beliefs* (Report No. 15). Urbana, IL: Center on Families, Communities, Schools, and Children's Learning, Illinois University. (ERIC Document Service No. ED362271).

Blumenkrantz, D. G. (1992). *Fulfilling the promise of children's services.* San Francisco: Jossey-Bass.

Charles, C. M. (2005). *Building classroom discipline* (8th ed.). Boston: Allyn & Bacon.

Fisher, R., & Ury, W. (1983). *Getting to yes.* New York: Penguin.

Greenwood, G. E., & Hickman, C. W. (1991). Research and practice in parent involvement: Implications for teacher education. *Elementary School Journal, 91*(3), 279–288.

Grolnick, W. S., Ryan, R. M., & Deci, E. L. (1991). Inner resources for school achievement: Motivational mediators of children's perceptions of their parents. *Journal of Educational Psychology, 83*(4), 508–517.

Grolnick, W. S., & Slowiaczek, M. L. (1994). Parents' involvement in children's schooling: A multidimensional conceptualization and motivational model. *Child Development, 65,* 237–252.

Henderson, A. T., & Berla, N. (1994). *A new generation of evidence: The family is critical to student achievement.* Columbia, MD: National Committee for Citizens in Education.

Hoover-Dempsey, K. V., & Sandler, H. M. (1997). Why do parents become involved in their children's education? *Review of Educational Research, 67*(1), 3–42.

Jehl, J., & Kirst, M. (1991). Getting ready to provide school-linked services: What schools must do. *The Future of Children, 2*(1), 95–106.

Keith, T. Z., Reimers, T. M., Fehrmann, P. G., Pottebaum, S. M., & Aubey, L. W. (1986). Parental involvement, homework, and TV time: Direct and indirect effects on high school achievement. *Journal of Educational Psychology, 78*(5), 373–380.

Knitzer, J., & Page, S. (1995). *Mapping and tracking initiatives to meet the needs of young children and families: A state-by-state overview.* New York: National Center for Children in Poverty.

Melaville, A. I., & Blank, M. J. (1991). *What it takes*. Washington, DC: Education and Human Services Consortium.

Milliea, S., & Coleman, M. T. (1992). Creating a sense of community: The Austin School of the Future. In W. H. Holtzman (Ed.), *School of the future*. Austin, TX: Hogg Foundation for Mental Health.

22. Classroom Management: Baumrind Styles/Teacher Efficacy (Grades 3–5)

Ashton, P. (1984, Sept/Oct.) Teacher efficacy: A motivational paradigm for effective teacher education. *Journal of Teacher Education, 28–32*.

Bowman, R. (1983, November). Effective classroom management: A primer for practicing professionals. *The Clearing House, 116–118*.

Brophy, J. (1983). Classroom organization and management. *The Elementary School Journal, 83*(4), 265–285.

Brophy, J. (1985, Fall). Classroom management as instruction: Socializing self-guidance in students. *Theory Into Practice, 233–240*.

Charles, C. M. (2005). *Building classroom discipline* (8th ed.). Boston: Allyn & Bacon.

Cornell, N. (1986, September). Encouraging responsibility—A discipline plan that works. *Learning 86, 47–49*.

Curwin, R., & Mendler, A. (1988, October). Packaged discipline programs: Let the buyer beware. *Educational Leadership, 46*(1), 68–73.

Curwin, R., & Mendler, A. (1989, March). We repeat, let the buyer beware: A response to Canter. *Educational Leadership, 46*(6), 83.

Evertson, C. (1989). Classroom organization and management. In M. Reynolds (Ed.), *Knowledge base for the beginning teacher* (pp. 59–70). New York: Pergamon Press.

Evertson, C., & Emmer, E. (1982). Preventive classroom management. In D. Duke (Ed.), *Helping teachers manage classrooms* (pp. 2–31). Alexandria, VA: Association for Supervision and Curriculum Development.

Kindsvatter, R., & Levine, M. (1980, June). The myths of discipline. *Phi Delta Kappan, 690–693*.

McCormack, S. (1989, March). Response to Render, Padilla, and Krank: But practitioners say it works! *Educational Leadership, 46*(6), 77–79.

McDaniel, T. (1989, March). The discipline debate: A road through the thicket. *Educational Leadership, 46*(6), 81–82.

Randolph, C., & Evertson, C. (1994, Spring). Images of management for learner-centered classrooms. *Action in Teacher Education, 55–64*.

Render, G., Padilla, J., & Krank, H. (1989, March). What research really shows about assertive discipline. *Educational Leadership, 46*(6), 72–75.

Van Houten, R., & Doleys, D. M. (1983). Are social reprimands effective? In S. Axelrod & J. Apsche (Eds.), *The effects of punishment on human behavior.* San Diego: Academic Press.

23. Instruction: Learner- vs. Teacher-Centered (Grades 9–12)

Cobb, P. (1994). Where is the mind? Constructivist and sociocultural perspectives on mathematical development. *Educational Researcher, 23*(7), 13–20.

Cobb, P., & Yackel, R. (1996). Constructivist, emergent, and sociocultural perspectives in the context of developmental research. *Educational Psychologist, 31,* 175–190.

Charles, C. M. (2005). *Building classroom discipline* (8th ed.). Boston: Allyn & Bacon.

Flynn, L. (1989, May). Developing critical reading skills through cooperative problem solving. *The Reading Teacher,* 664–668.

Kohn, A. (1987, October). It's hard to get left out of a pair. *Psychology Today,* 53–57.

Pearson, C. (1979, March). Cooperative learning: An alternative to cheating and failure. *Learning,* 34–37.

Prawat, R. S. (1996). Constructivism, modern and postmodern. *Educational Psychologist, 31,* 215–225.

Rosenshine, B. (1979). Content, time, and direct instruction. In P. Peterson & H. Walberg (Eds.), *Research on teaching.* Berkeley, CA: McCutchen Publishing.

Rosenshine, B., & Stevens, R. (1986). Research on teaching. *Handbook of research on teaching.* (3rd ed.) (pp. 376–391). New York: Macmillan.

Slavin, R. (1984). Students motivating students to excel: Cooperative incentives, cooperative tasks, and student achievement. *The Elementary School Journal, 85*(1), 53–64.

Slavin, R. (1987, November). Cooperative learning and the cooperative school. *Educational Leadership,* 7–13.

Slavin, R. (1988, April). Cooperative learning and individualized instruction. *The Education Digest,* 23–25.

Slavin, R. (1989). Comprehensive cooperative learning models for heterogeneous classrooms. *The Pointer, 33*(2), 12–18.

Slavin, R. (1991). Cooperative learning and group contingencies. *Journal of Behavioral Education, 1*(1), 105–115.

Topping, K. (1989, March). Peer tutoring and paired reading: Combining two powerful techniques. *The Reading Teacher,* 488–494.

Wells, A. (1996). Situated action, symbol systems and universal computation. *Minds and Machines, 6,* 33–46.

Assessment and Evaluation

24. *Standardized Tests: Evaluating, Interpreting, Aptitude vs. Achievement, Teacher's Role and Issues and Controversies (Grades K–5)*

Bond, L. (1995). Critical issue: Rethinking assessment and its role in supporting educational reform. Oak Brook, IL: North Central Regional Educational Laboratory. *Mathematics Teacher, 85,* 16–21.

Bond, L. (1996). Norm- and criterion-referenced testing. *Practical Assessment, Research & Evaluation, 5*(2).

Brualdi, A. (1998). *Implementing performance assessment in the classroom.* Washington, DC: ERIC Clearinghouse on Assessment and Evaluation, from ED423312.

Canady, R., & Hotchkiss, P. (1989, September). It's a good score! Just a bad grade. *Phi Delta Kappan,* 68–71.

Cizek, G. (1991, May). Innovation or enervation? Performance assessment in perspective. *Phi Delta Kappan,* 695–699.

Dubert, L. (1987, February). Two ideas for grading simulations and higher level thinking activities. *The Clearing House,* 266–269.

Grigorenko, E. L., & Sternberg, R. J. (1998). Dynamic testing. *Psychological Bulletin, 124,* 75–111.

Merwin, J. (1989). Evaluation. In M. Reynolds (Ed.), *Knowledge base for the beginning teacher.* New York: Pergamon Press.

Popham, W. J. (1980, April). Educational measurement for the improvement of instruction. *Phi Delta Kappan,* 531–534.

Ryan, K., & Levine, J. (1981). Impact of academic performance pattern on assigned grade and predicted performance. *Journal of Educational Psychology, 73*(3), 386–392.

Shepard, L. (1979, Fall). Norm-referenced vs. criterion-referenced tests. *Educational Horizons,* 26–35.

Stallings, J., & Krasavage, E. (1986). Program implementation and student achievement in a four-year Madeline Hunter Follow-Through project. *The Elementary School Journal, 87*(2), 117–138.

Terwilliger, J. (1989). Classroom standard setting and grading practices. *Educational Measurement: Issues and Practices, 8*(2), 15–19.

Walberg, H. (1990, February). Productive teaching and instruction: Assessing the knowledge base. *Phi Delta Kappan,* 470–478.

Wiggins, G. (1989). Teaching to the (authentic) test. *Educational Leadership, 46*(7), 41–47.

25. Classroom Assessments: Traditional vs. Alternative, Formative vs. Summative, Evaluating, Traditional vs. Alternative Assessments (Grades 9–12)

American Educational Research Association. (2000). *AERA position statement concerning high-stakes testing in PreK-12 education.* Washington, DC: Author. Retrieved from www.aera.net/about/policy/stakes.htm.

Bond, L. (1995). Critical issue: Rethinking assessment and its role in supporting educational reform. Oak Brook, IL: North Central Regional Educational Laboratory. *Mathematics Teacher, 85,* 16–21.

Bond, L. (1996). Norm- and criterion-referenced testing. *Practical Assessment, Research & Evaluation, 5*(2), 51–57.

Brualdi, A. (1998). *Implementing performance assessment in the classroom.* Washington, DC: ERIC Clearinghouse on Assessment and Evaluation, from ED423312.

Baker, E. (1984, March). Can educational research inform educational practice? Yes! *Phi Delta Kappan,* 453–455.

Canady, R., & Hotchkiss, P. (1989, September). It's a good score! Just a bad grade. *Phi Delta Kappan,* 68–71.

Cizek, G. (1991, May). Innovation or enervation? Performance assessment in perspective. *Phi Delta Kappan,* 695–699.

Dietel, R., Herman, J., & Knuth, R. (1991). *What does research say about assessment?* Oak Brook, IL: North Central Regional Educational Laboratory. Retrieved from www.ncrel.org/ncrel/sdrs/areas/stw_esys/4assess.htm.

Eisner, E. (1999). The uses and limits of performance assessment. *Phi Delta Kappan, 80*(5). Retrieved from www.pdkintl.org/kappan/keis9905.htm.

Elliott, S. (1995). *Creating meaningful performance assessments.* Reston, VA: Council for Exceptional Children, ERIC Clearinghouse on Disabilities and Gifted Education, from ED381985.

Frary, R. (1995). More multiple-choice item writing do's and don'ts. *Practical Assessment, Research & Evaluation, 4*(11), 695–699.

Shepard, L. (1979, Fall). Norm-referenced vs. criterion-referenced tests. *Educational Horizons,* 26–35.

Terwilliger, J. (1989). Classroom standard setting and grading practices. *Educational Measurement: Issues and Practices, 8*(2), 15–19.

Walberg, H. (1990, February). Productive teaching and instruction: Assessing the knowledge base. *Phi Delta Kappan,* 470–478.

Wiggins, G. (1989). Teaching to the (authentic) test. *Educational Leadership, 46*(7), 41–47.

Worthen, B., & Spandel, V. (1991). Putting the standardized test debate in perspective, *Educational Leadership, 48*(5), 65–69.